D0504845

Branch
Lines of
Berkshire

Branch Lines of Berkshire

COLIN G. MAGGS

First published in the United Kingdom by Berkshire Books

Copyright © Colin G. Maggs, 1993

All rights reserved. No part of this publication may be reproduced, stored in a retrieval system, or transmitted, in any form or by any means, electronic, mechanical, photocopying, recording or otherwise, without the prior permission of the publishers and copyright holder.

BERKSHIRE BOOKS
Publishing imprint of Berkshire County Council
In collaboration with
Alan Sutton Publishing Ltd
Phoenix Mill · Far Thrupp · Stroud
Gloucestershire

Alan Sutton Publishing Inc.
83 Washington Street · Dover · NH 03820

British Library Cataloguing in Publication Data

Maggs, Colin G.
Branch Lines of Berkshire
I. Title
385.09422

ISBN 0-7509-0316-3

Library of Congress Cataloging-in-Publication data applied for

Jacket photographs. Front: 14XX class 0–4–2T No. 1444 in lined green livery at Wallingford, soon after its arrival from Cholsey and Moulsford. Typically a bucket hangs from a lamp bracket. The driver, having walked back from the control vestibule of the auto trailer, grasps the hand rail and has a word with his fireman, who is in the cab. A postman drags a couple of heavy mailbags along the platform, having removed them from the luggage compartment, the doors of which stand open. The double corrugated-iron shed at the far end of the platform was used as a bicycle shed. In the right foreground is a platform seat with the GWR monogram on the legs, and above is a gas lamp. Behind the coach is the engine shed, while in the top right-hand corner is the water tower. (*c.* 1957, M.E.J. Deane.) *Back*: Lambourn, seen from the buffer stops. 57XX class 0–6–0PT No. 4666 stands at the foot of the water tower while running round the ex-LMS coach in order to couple on to the far end for the return journey. There is no corridor gangway blank door. A postman wheels a pair of trucks along the platform, presumably having placed mail in the coach's luggage compartment. The siding on the far right is on the site of the locomotive shed of 1937. The nearest wagon is a Cordon gas cylinder wagon, used for charging the gas-lit horse boxes. A surprising number of coaches are in the yard beyond.

Typeset in 9/10 Palatino.
Typesetting and origination by
Alan Sutton Publishing Limited.
Printed and bound in Great Britain by
Butler & Tanner Ltd, Frome and London

Contents

KEY

- Great Western Railway
- London and South Western Railway
- South Eastern Railway
- Station open 1993
- Station closed 1993

0 5 10 miles

OXFORDSHIRE

SURREY

Handborough
Cassington Halt
Eynsham
South Leigh
Witney
Carterton
Alvescot
Kelmscott and Langford
Brize Norton and Bampton
Fairford
Lechlade
Highworth
Stanton
Hannington
Stratton
Stratton Park Halt
SWINDON
Shrivenham
Faringdon
Uffington
Challow
Wantage Tramway
Grove Bridge
Wantage
Wantage Road

Yarnton
Wolvercote Platform
OXFORD
Iffley
Hinksey Halt
Morris Cowley
Littlemore
Abingdon Road
Radley
Abingdon Junction
Abingdon
Culham
Appleford
Steventon
DIDCOT
Upton and Blewbury
Wallingford
Cholsey
Moulsford

BERKSHIRE

Lambourn
Eastbury
East Garston
Great Shefford
Welford Park
Boxford
Speen
Newbury West Fields
Stockcross and Bagnor
Halt
Kintbury
Hungerford
Bedwyn
NEWBURY
Woodhay
Highclere
Burghclere
Midgham
Thatcham
Hermitage
Pinewood Halt
Hampstead Norris
Compton
Churn
Aldermaston
Theale
Goring and Streatley
Pangbourne
Tilehurst
Reading West

HAMPSHIRE

Bramley
Mortimer

Henley-on-Thames
Shiplake
Wargrave
Twyford
Earley
Winnersh Triangle
Winnersh
Wokingham
first Reading South
second Reading South
READING

High Wycombe
Penn Halt
Wycombe West
Loudwater
Bourne End
Wooburn Green
Marlow
Cookham
Furze Platt
Boyne Hill
Maidenhead
Taplow
Burnham
Slough
Chalvey Halt
Datchet
Windsor and Eton Riverside
Windsor and Eton Central
Sunnymead
Wraysbury
Sunningdale
Ascot
Ascot West
Bagshot
Camberley
Frimley
Farnborough North
Blackwater
second Sandhurst
first Sandhurst
Crowthorne
Bracknell
Martins Heron

WILTSHIRE

BRANCH LINES OF BERKSHIRE

Introduction

Most of the branch lines of Berkshire were associated with the Great Western Railway. Receiving its Act in 1835, granting powers to build a line from London to Bristol, the GWR opened to Maidenhead on 4 June 1838, Twyford (1 July 1839), Reading (30 March 1840), Steventon (1 June 1840), Faringdon Road (later named Challow) on 20 July 1840 and throughout to Bristol on 30 June 1841.

From Reading a principal branch, the Berks and Hants Railway, ran to Southcote Junction south-west of Reading, where the line split: one fork running to Basingstoke and the other to Newbury and Hungerford. The latter was eventually improved and upgraded, and in 1906 became part of a new direct line to the West of England.

Another principal branch was the Didcot, Newbury and Southampton Railway which ran north to south through the county and, as well as serving the local community, carried trains from the Midlands to the south coast.

On either side of the Great Western main line were towns which demanded a railway, and these were served by branches. Usually built by independent companies, it proved difficult to run the lines at a profit and within a few years they were sold to the GWR, usually at a loss to their shareholders. In due course, with the development of road transport, these short branches proved uncompetitive and most were closed by the mid-1960s.

Although the GWR was the railway which covered most of Berkshire, it did not hold a monopoly. The South Eastern Railway tapped the lucrative Reading traffic in 1849, the London and South Western Railway, with running powers over the South Eastern Railway, providing a third route to London in 1856. The former SER line to Reading was electrified in 1939, but apart from this the other Berkshire branches used steam or diesel traction.

The county boundary followed in this book is that of Berkshire before the 1974 revision, and the branches are described in order from east to west.

Grateful thanks are due to John Hayward for checking and improving the text and captions.

Key To Maps

——	Great Western Railway
╫╫╫╫	London and South Western Railway
✳✳✳✳	South Eastern Railway
—○—	Station open 1993
—●—	Station closed 1993

Slough to Windsor

When the GWR was planned in 1835, a branch was proposed to Windsor, but Eton College made objections. The provost wrote, 'No public good whatever could possibly come from such an undertaking', and this violent opposition caused the line to be dropped from the GWR's Act. When an Act for building a line to Windsor was eventually granted in 1848, the college was protected by various clauses. The branch opened on 8 October 1849, before the works were fully complete, so as to steal a march on the London and South Western Railway whose line to an independent station, Windsor and Eton Riverside, was not opened until 1 December 1849. The GWR branch was on the broad gauge, a third rail being added in March 1862 to accommodate standard gauge rolling stock. The line was possibly unique in running mixed gauge passenger trains, the stock of different gauges being connected by 'match' vehicles. The broad gauge was removed on 30 June 1883.

Slough station in Buckinghamshire, the junction with the main line, was – like Reading and Taunton – of Brunel's peculiar one-sided variety, with platforms for 'Up' and 'Down' trains both situated on the 'Down' side of the track. This plan avoided passengers having to cross the tracks, but led to delays when trains were not keeping to the timetable. With the increase in traffic the system became quite impossible to work and the twin stations were replaced in 1886 by a main building on the 'Down' side, with island and 'Up' Relief platforms. Above the cornice of the main building were three curved French pavilion roofs, each capped with French-style iron railings. What appear to be fish-scale tiles are actually metal. This fine building was designed by J. Danks. Bay platforms at the west end were provided between the Main and Relief lines, and also by the 'Down' Main platform, for Windsor branch shuttle trains. On the 'Up' side a memorial was erected to 'Station Jim', a dog who collected £40 for the GWR Widows' and Orphans' Fund until his death in 1896.

Unlike the other Berkshire branches off the quadruple track, which only had access to and from the relief lines, the Windsor branch had through running to and from the main lines as well. The crossover to and from the Relief line was taken out of use on 29 September 1963. The branch left immediately west of the station and a triangular junction allowed trains to run through to Windsor from either the east or west.

Until 1900 the West Loop was only used by royal specials and race trains, but during that year it was used by two regular 'Down' trains to Basingstoke and one 'Up'. Within the triangle was the carriage shed and permanent way yard, the engine shed being adjacent to the East Loop, and one of the first locomotive sheds on the GWR. Built of timber, it was replaced by a two-road brick shed in 1868, enlarged to four roads in 1872 and closed on 1 June 1964. Since 9 September 1963 the track beyond Bath Road Junction, formerly the southern apex of the triangle, has been single, the 'Up' line having been lifted. On the same date the West Loop was also singled, the remaining line being taken out of use on 25 July 1970.

About half a mile beyond Bath Road Junction was Chalvey Halt, opened on 6 May 1929 and closed on 6 July 1930. It was not a complete waste of shareholders' cash as the platforms were re-erected in Gloucestershire at Cashes Green, near Stroud. Beyond the halt was a siding which until 27 January 1952 brought coal to the Slough and Datchet Electric Light Company. The last 2,035 yd of the branch is on Windsor Viaduct, which incorporates the bridge carrying the branch over the Thames into Berkshire. This bridge, which has a 203 ft span of wrought-iron bowstring design, crosses the river on the skew and is Brunel's oldest surviving railway bridge. Originally supported on six cast-iron cylinders, these were later replaced by brick abutments. At first the approach arches on the Slough side were timber, but these were later replaced by brick. The bridge is a Grade II listed structure.

The first Windsor station, constructed of timber, was really a standard GWR train shed, but because of its exalted position near Windsor Castle, was distinguished by a row of windows at the end to raise the roof level. It accommodated two roads and a central carriage road, and two short, narrow platforms. The station was not really spacious enough for royal occasions and, as a Diamond Jubilee present from the GWR to Queen Victoria, a special royal station was built a road-width from a new public station, a covered entrance spanning the driveway separating the two. The entrance arch of brick and stone carried the GWR coat of arms and the windscreen below had the words 'Great Western Railway' in ornate brass lettering. The wide platform of the royal station was spanned by a glazed train shed, 'To keep my soldiers dry' as requested by the queen. The platform was spacious enough to turn the royal carriage and accommodate a full military escort either mounted or on foot.

Within this train shed was the royal waiting room, built in the standard GWR style of the period but faced with stone instead of brick. It had a wood-panelled dado and was lit by an Art Nouveau dome. First used on 21 June 1897, this royal waiting room only contained ladies' accommodation, so following the accession of King Edward VII, it was enlarged in 1902 at a cost of £1,705 to provide facilities for gentlemen. The same year incandescent gas lighting was provided throughout the public and royal stations for £108.

The new public station, built 1895–7, had two platforms and an island allowing a total of four roads plus a short bay on the south side. On one side was the arrival platform and on the other the departure, the island platforms serving both 'Up' and 'Down' trains. The island platform had no shelter until 1908, when a canopy was provided at a cost of £1,870.

The buildings were in dark-red brick relieved with limestone string courses. The splendid entrance hall was well-lit with windows and 150 candle power gas lamps. On 17 November 1968 platforms 3 and 4 were taken out of use, followed by platform 2 from 5 September 1969. Today the station is protected as a Grade II building. In 1982 BR and Madame Tussaud's restored the station, including the royal waiting room, and opened the Royalty and Railways exhibition in 1983, renamed Royalty and Empire the following year. It includes a replica of the Royal Train: 'Achilles' class 4–2–2 No. 3041 *The Queen* and two royal saloons, one a former royal vehicle rescued from use as a holiday bungalow in Wales.

The station has had three names. Simply Windsor until 1 June 1904, it then became Windsor and Eton, with the suffix Central being added on 26 September 1949.

When the passenger station was enlarged in 1895–7, due to its position on a viaduct most of the existing goods yard had to be taken over to provide sufficient land. Only the goods shed remained on the same level as the passenger station, a new six-road goods yard with a capacity of 170 wagons being built with access down a 1 in 45 gradient. For reasons of safety, loads were restricted to twenty wagons and subject to a speed limit of 5 mph. The branch closed to goods on 6 January 1964.

Until the 1890s almost all trains were shuttles to and from Slough, but generally with a through coach to or from Paddington attached. In the 1860s one train daily from Windsor actually slipped a coach into Paddington, it being a rare, if not unique feature to do this into a principal terminus. Just after this train passed Royal Oak, it slipped a coach for the main-line station at Paddington. This free-wheeled behind the rest of the train, gradually decreasing its speed and just giving the signalman time to shift the points to turn it into a main platform after the passage of the rest of the train to Bishop's Road station and the Metropolitan Railway. In later years the Board of Trade would have frowned at such a dangerous procedure.

From the mid-1890s most Windsor trains ran through to London, thus avoiding any coupling on to a main-line train. They ran not only to Paddington, but to Aldgate, Victoria (London, Chatham and Dover Railway station), or by the West Loop to Basingstoke. Fifteen of these 'Up' trains were 'fast', covering the distance between Windsor and London in thirty-two to forty minutes. The service covered most of the day, 'Down' trains running from 5.40 a.m. until midnight. Some main-line expresses slipped Windsor vehicles at Slough. Today the service is frequent with thirty-eight trains each way, but as a change of trains is necessary at Slough, the fastest services take thirty-two minutes.

Beginning with Queen Victoria, the Windsor branch has conveyed every British sovereign on his or her last journey. For the funeral of King George V on 28 January 1936, for example, the ordinary train service on the branch was entirely suspended from 10.30 a.m. until 6 p.m. Five special trains were booked to carry invited guests from Paddington to Windsor and scheduled to cover the distance in thirty minutes. Guests did not hold railway tickets but were carried on production of their invitation cards. The 4–6–0 No. 4082 *Windsor Castle* hauled the black-painted funeral saloon. No. 4082 bore the royal crown-topped headlamps and carried the coat of arms made at Swindon Works in 1897 and first used on the Royal Train on the occasion of Queen Victoria's Diamond Jubilee.

On arrival at Windsor, the locomotives used for the Royal Train and the special guest train ahead of it, were taken at once to Slough for turning via the triangle, before returning immediately to Windsor. The engines of the other guest specials were turned and held at Slough shed until required.

For the funeral of King George VI on 15 February 1952, No. 4082 *Windsor Castle* was unavailable as it was at Swindon Works being overhauled. It was felt, however, that it would be a fitting tribute to King George VI if the engine of his funeral train bore the same name as that used on the occasion of the funeral of his father, so the name and number-plates of No. 4082 were transferred to No. 7013 *Bristol Castle*.

Around 1911 the Windsor branch was the scene of trials by the GWR of No. 100, a very early internal-combustion engined vehicle. Designed by the British Thompson-Houston Company Limited, it had a 40 hp Maudslay petrol engine which drove a dynamo, the current generated powering two electric motors on the axles. The radiator stood vertically on the roof. The railcar had two braking systems: hand and compressed air. A contemporary writer recorded:

The journey between Slouth [sic] and Windsor was about 2½ miles in length; the timetable allowed 9 minutes and no difficulty was experienced in adhering to it, despite fairly heavy gradients. A maximum speed of 32 miles per hour was obtained. On petrol, the consumption worked out at about 8 miles per gallon with a range of 240 miles, a creditable performance, bearing in mind that the vehicle weighed 14 tons 9 cwts. The overall length was 33 feet 3 inches, which allowed seating accommodation for up to 46 persons. Two staff only were required to run the vehicle – a driver and a guard.

The GWR withdrew No. 100 in October 1919 and sold it to Lever Brothers Limited, Port Sunlight, Cheshire, for use on that company's system.

Accidents on the GWR were rare and it was strange that Slough was the scene of two major crashes within six months at the turn of the century, the coincidence being made greater by the fact that both involved a Windsor branch and West of England trains, and both occurred on a Saturday.

The first took place on the day before Christmas Eve 1899 and was reported in the ordinary Christmas Day editions of the daily papers. There was thick fog that morning as the 5.47 a.m. from Windsor, running about half an hour late, crossed the main line into Slough station to gain the 'Up' Relief. At the same time the 'Up' mail from Plymouth and Bristol, running an hour late and double-headed by 'Achilles' class 4–2–2 No. 3076 *Princess Beatrice* and No. 3071 *Emlyn* of the same class, crashed through the branch train. Surprisingly, and thankfully at this time of year, there were no fatalities and only one passenger was injured. Passengers at the rear of the express did not even feel the impact and, until they were told the reason, were furious at the delay. A purse and a Christmas turkey were lost in the wreckage – neither was recovered.

The *Berkshire Chronicle* of 30 December 1899 tells of the clearing-up operations:

> Stationmaster Mr Pearse, Supt Turner of the Permanent Way Department, Chief of Locomotive Staff Mr Walter Guest, and a strong breakdown gang got to work and in about two hours the carriages of the Mail train were liberated and sent on to Paddington, together with a portion of the Travelling Post Office. The Up Main and Down Main, and Down Relief were blocked. Up traffic went via the Up Relief, Down traffic via the Windsor branch and on to the main line via the West curve. The accident disorganized the Christmas and ordinary traffic between Paddington and the West to a serious extent, taking 6 or 7 hours from London to Slough, Windsor and Maidenhead. The breakdown gang worked all night and during Sunday and during a portion of Christmas Day clearing the wreckage and returning the enormous engines to the metals.

The paper gives a clue to the cause of the accident: 'The fog rose so rapidly that there was not time to get the foggers out on the Saturday evening, and the drivers could not see the signals.'

The second Slough crash happened on 16 June 1900. The eight-coach 1.05 p.m. Paddington to Windsor, well-filled with racegoers and running non-stop from Paddington, arrived at Slough at 1.30 p.m. to allow Slough passengers to alight and tickets to be collected from the passengers for Windsor, the latter station being 'open'. Two minutes after it had halted, a 'Down' express running through danger signals approached at full speed on the same line. A porter ran along the track towards it waving a warning and the signalman with a red flag leaned out of his box. People on the platform yelled to passengers in the coaches of the Windsor train to jump out to save their lives, and many took this advice, reducing the death toll 'Achilles' class 4–2–2 No. 3015 *Kennet* struck the rear of the Windsor train, smashing the last three coaches, the underframes being pushed up to demolish both the foot-bridge and platform canopy. To add to the disaster, the timber-bodied carriages ignited. Five passengers died and thirty-five were seriously injured.

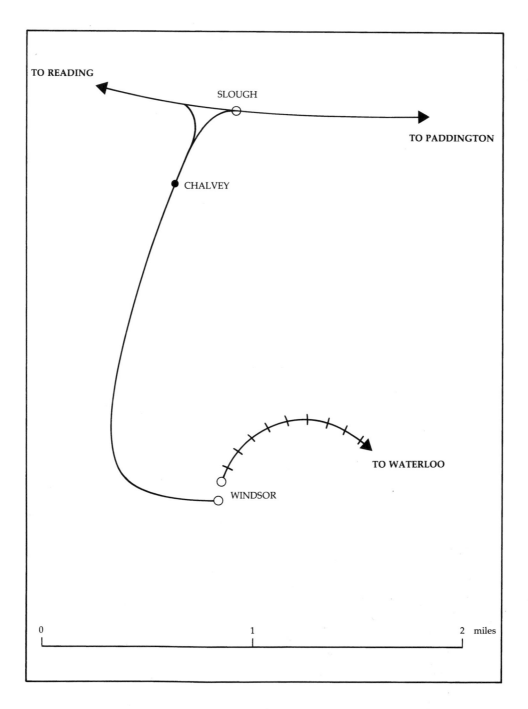

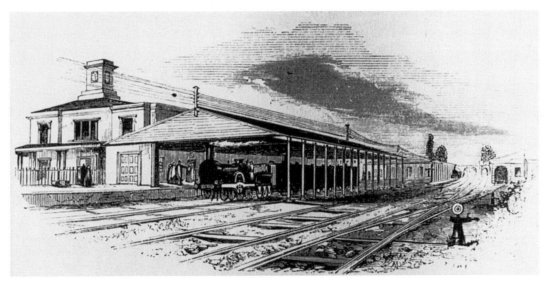

The 'Up' station at Slough with a passing train hauled by a 2–2–2 locomotive nearest the artist and the 'Down' station beyond. To the right is the goods shed. The Windsor branch curved left at its far end.

c. 1852 George Measom

14XX class 0–4–2T No. 1450 carrying an 81B (Slough) shed-plate in the Windsor branch bay platform at Slough. It is attached to an auto-trailer. No. 1450 is preserved on the South Devon Railway.

24.1.54 Frank J. Saunders

'Achilles' class 4–2–2 No. 3015 *Kennet* after colliding with the rear of the Paddington to Windsor racegoers' train at Slough. Notice the wreckage piled towards the foot-bridge and platform canopy.
16.6.1900 Author's collection

Ex-GWR diesel railcar No. W13W leaving the Windsor branch bay, Slough.
April 1954 Frank J. Saunders

Ex-LMS class 6P5F 2–6–0 No. 42781 on the return ten-coach excursion from Windsor and Eton Central to Nuneaton on the Slough West Curve. This was the only known visit of an engine of this class to the branch.

6.7.60 Frank J. Saunders

Ex-GWR railcars Nos W31W and W21W approaching Slough locomotive shed from Windsor on the last Saturday that these vehicles worked the branch.

1958 Frank J. Saunders

View from the cab of ex-GWR railcar No. W13W crossing Brunel's oldest surviving railway bridge en route from Windsor to Slough.

27.3.54 Frank J. Saunders

View from the cab of a diesel railcar arriving at Windsor station. A 2–6–2T stands ready to leave. To the far right is the framework of a gasholder.

1957 Frank J. Saunders

Postcard view of the concourse of Windsor station at the ends of platforms 3 and 4. Note the two lines of lamps at the stop blocks.

c. 1905 Author's collection

The entrance archway to Windsor station. Note the Jubilee date 1897, clock and GWR coat of arms. The open-top double-decker buses are also of interest.

c. 1905 Author's collection

The train shed at Windsor and Eton. As the track is mixed gauge, the picture must have been drawn in March 1862 or later. Note that for coaches to be close to the platform, the rail common to both gauges was on the platform side. In the foreground is Windsor viaduct. Windsor Castle and St George's Chapel can be seen on the hill to the left.

c. 1862 Author's collection

A DMU leaving Platform 2 at Windsor and Eton Central for Slough. Although platforms 3 and 4 on the right were still usable, the rails appear to be rusty, while the paving slabs in the foreground are cracked and in a dangerous condition.

9.3.68 E. Wilmshurst

Members of the Didcot branch of the British Legion at Windsor on the occasion of King George VI's funeral.

15.2.52 Author's collection

An attempt was made by Roderick Maclean to shoot Queen Victoria as her carriage left Windsor station. Superintendent Hayes on the left is about to arrest the would-be assassin.

2.3.1882 *The Graphic*

The scene at the station immediately before the attack: a) Roderick Maclean, the attacker; b) broken line showing the direction of the shot; c) Superintendent Hayes, who arrested Maclean; d) Maclean. The goods shed is on the left.

2.3.1882 *The Graphic*

The accommodation plan for Queen Victoria's funeral train.

2.2.1901

GREAT WESTERN RAILWAY.

FUNERAL

OF

Her late Majesty Queen Victoria

On SATURDAY, FEBRUARY 2nd, 1901,

The Train Service throughout the Great Western Company's system will be the same as on Sundays, with the following modifications, viz.:—

The 5.30 a.m. and 5.40 a.m. Newspaper Trains from Paddington will run as usual as far as Plymouth and Swansea respectively, with connections to the Weymouth Line, Torquay, Kingswear and Penzance, and also to Oxford, Birmingham, Wolverhampton, Dudley, Worcester, Malvern, &c.

The 12.0 night Train from Paddington to Penzance, and the 12.15 night Train from Paddington to Birmingham, Chester, Birkenhead and Liverpool will run as usual.

LONDON AND WINDSOR SERVICE.

The 1.0 p.m. Sunday Train from Paddington to Windsor will not run.

The 10.30 a.m., 10.35 a.m., 1.50 p.m. and 2.20 p.m. Sunday Trains from Paddington will not convey passengers to Windsor.

Windsor Station will be closed for public traffic from 11.0 a.m. until 2.30 p.m.

LONDON SUBURBAN SERVICE.

The following Trains will run as on Week Days in addition to the usual Sunday service :—

8.0 a.m. Southall to Paddington.
7.45 a.m. Windsor to Paddington.
8.0 a.m. Reading to Paddington.
8.50 a.m. Southall to Paddington.
8.53 a.m. Uxbridge to Paddington.

A Train will run from Southall to Paddington at 10.0 a.m., calling at intermediate Stations.

The 11.25 a.m. Sunday Train from High Wycombe to Paddington will be half an hour later at all Stations.

SAILINGS—NEW MILFORD AND WATERFORD.

There will be no Steamer from Waterford to New Milford on Friday, February 1st, nor from New Milford to Waterford on Sunday morning, February 3rd.

The issue of Week-end Excursion Tickets to Windsor and the Half-day Excursion Tickets to London will be suspended.

For particulars of any additional Local arrangements on other parts of the Line, see Special announcements issued locally.

J. L. WILKINSON, General Manager.

Paddington Station, January, 1901.

A handbill giving modifications to GWR train services on the day of Queen Victoria's funeral.
2.2.1901

Maidenhead to Cookham

The line from Maidenhead to Cookham was built as part of the Wycombe Railway which received its Act on 27 July 1846, authorizing a line from Maidenhead to Aylesbury via High Wycombe. This broad gauge single line was laid with 90½ lb per yd Barlow rails. In section these looked like an inverted 'V' with ends a foot apart. They were not laid on sleepers like conventional rail, but the 'V' was packed with ballast to prevent movement. These rails were not a success as the gauge had a tendency to spread. They had been patented in 1849 by William Henry Barlow, engineer to the Midland Railway and later responsible for building St Pancras station which, at 240 ft, had the largest roof span in Britain.

The line from Maidenhead through Cookham to High Wycombe opened on 1 August 1854, the line being leased to the GWR. It was extended from High Wycombe to Thame on 1 August 1862, Princes Risborough to Aylesbury 1 October 1863 and Thame to Oxford on 24 October 1864. The Wycombe Railway was amalgamated with the GWR from 1 February 1867. Between 23 and 31 August 1870 it was converted to standard gauge, passenger traffic recommencing on 1 September and goods a few days later.

The first station at Maidenhead, opened on 4 June 1838, close to the Dumb Bell bridge over the Bath Road, formed a railhead from which road coaches were transferred to or from rail. Its timber buildings high on the sides of the new embankment were surmounted by a clock tower; weight precluded a stone or brick structure. In August 1838 the directors resolved to move the station a mile westwards as soon as the line had been extended and it ceased to be a temporary terminus, but this intention had not been carried out when the branch to High Wycombe opened. Branch trains also called at the single-platform Maidenhead (Wycombe branch) station, later Maidenhead (Boyne Hill), situated a short distance from Wycombe Junction and about 2 miles west of the then main-line Maidenhead station. The latter was renamed Taplow on 1 May 1869 to avoid confusion with the Wycombe Railway's station at Boyne Hill.

The present Maidenhead station immediately east of Wycombe Junction opened on 1 November 1871, when Boyne Hill became redundant. The renamed Maidenhead station remained open until 31 August 1872, a new Taplow station being opened the following day. The new Maidenhead station, situated on an embankment, had its offices at road level. When the line was quadrupled in 1893 two additional platforms were built, bringing the total to five. A new goods shed was provided at the same time. In 1926 the station was further improved with larger platform canopies, a refreshment room, parcels office, luggage subway and lifts. The branch platform was sheltered by a simple train shed – just a roof with no ends. During wet weather, if a passenger engine required water, the train had to be left in the shed while the engine uncoupled and ran forward to the water column. There is direct access to the branch from the bay platform and from the 'Up' and 'Down' Relief lines. The branch junction was singled on 21 October 1974, the 'Down' line being lifted.

The extension of Slough Multiple Aspect Signalling (MAS) involved the closure of mechanical signal-boxes on 8 December 1963, a new flat-roofed box being provided to control the branch and its connections with the 'Up' and 'Down' Relief lines. In 1974 total control of the branch passed to Slough MAS. Maidenhead had closed to goods on 19 July 1965 but private-siding traffic continued.

Furze Platt station opened on 5 July 1937 at a cost of about £625. As a wartime measure it was unstaffed from 1 November 1942, but staff were later reinstated. The original timber platform was replaced with a concrete structure.

Cookham is a typical Wycombe Railway station of red brick and knapped flint. There were two platforms, the passing loop being brought into use on 2 May 1904. Due to the signal-box being sited on the north side of the level crossing, the guard of a 'Down' train crossing an 'Up' train at the station was required to telephone the signalman on arrival in order to report that the train had arrived complete without shedding any rolling stock, the signalman's view of the tail lamp being obstructed by the 'Up' train. The loop was taken out of use on 11 May 1969 and the signal-box was converted to a ground frame to control the level crossing until lifting barriers were installed in 1973. The only goods shed was a lock-up on the 'Up' platform. The foot-bridge had a glazed screen, but was demolished following the loop's removal. The cattle dock was economically built from bridge rails. The station closed to goods on 1 March 1965.

Beyond the station the line descends and about a mile beyond Cookham is the 44 yd long Cockmarsh Common viaduct over land liable to flooding, and a three-span, 162 yd long girder bridge across the Thames taking the branch out of Berkshire. Both these structures were originally built of timber.

From the first, through services ran from Paddington to High Wycombe, though some started from Maidenhead. In December 1872 the branch had eleven trains to London: nine to Paddington and two to Victoria. By 1893 a coach was slipped at Taplow from the 5.15 p.m. ex-Paddington and taken on to Maidenhead and Great Marlow. In 1933 the branch had thirteen 'Down' and twelve 'Up' trains, of which eleven 'Down' and eight 'Up' were to or from Paddington. Since 4 May 1970 trains have run from Maidenhead to Bourne End or Marlow only, as the line north of Bourne End is closed. Today the shuttle service on the branch offers twenty-one 'Down' trains and twenty-two 'Up'.

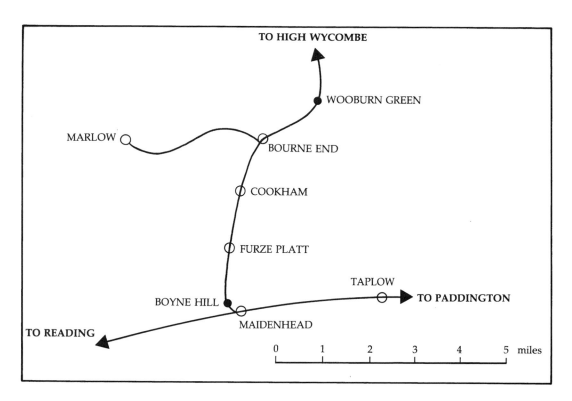

A broad gauge train hauled by a 2–2–2 locomotive arriving at the original Maidenhead station by the Dumb Bell bridge. Notice the timber buildings and board signal on the left. To the right is another board signal and, further right, the crossbar of a disc and crossbar signal. A disc displayed showed 'line clear' and a crossbar 'danger'. The board signal was painted red on one side and green on the other. Red indicated 'stop', while green warned 'caution' and was turned to indicate this three minutes after the passing of a train, until ten minutes after the passing of a passenger train (fifteen minutes for a goods train), when it was then changed to 'clear'.

c. 1852 George Measom

61XX class 2–6–2T No. 6143 at Maidenhead with the 6.14 p.m. (Sundays only) Maidenhead to High Wycombe service.

30.4.61 D. Holmes

Maidenhead signal-box opened on 8 December 1963 and closed on 21 October 1974. This style of architecture made the building soon look unkempt.

25.4.70 Derrick Payne

Maidenhead. Notice on the column of the 'Down' Relief platform water crane: 'Only tank engines working trains to Wycombe Branch must take water here. Tender engines must not take water. Oct 1901.'

18.2.61 Frank J. Saunders

North Town crossing signal-box, which adjoined Furze Platt Halt, doubled as a booking office. 14XX class 0–4–2T No. 1421 leaves, pushing the auto-coach to Maidenhead.

18.2.61 Frank J. Saunders

21

Furze Platt Halt, looking in the 'Up' direction, showing the timber-built platform with concrete fence posts. The waiting shelter is sited towards the far end of the platform where intending passengers entered via the ramp.

c. 1960 Lens of Sutton

14XX class 0–4–2T No. 1421 leaves Furze Platt Halt with the 10.39 a.m. Maidenhead to Marlow.

18.2.61 Frank J. Saunders

14XX class 0–4–2T No. 1421 enters Cookham with a Marlow to Maidenhead train. The driver stands in the vestibule of the auto-trailer, his hand on the brake. The signalman has promptly returned the signal to 'danger'. Just inside the open window of the signal-box is the wheel for operating the crossing gates.

25.3.61 Frank J. Saunders

The 1401 Marlow to Maidenhead service leaving Cookham. Set L205 comprised class 101 No. 54385 and class 117 No. 51367.

29.12.92 Author

The simple ticket office at Furze Platt. The path to the platform leads through the lean-to shelter. Just right of centre is a post supporting the level crossing warning lights with a notice below reading 'Keep Crossing Clear'. Further to the right is the raised barrier and the box containing its operating motor.

29.12.92 Author

The treadle at Furze Platt for a wheel flange to operate the level crossing barriers.

29.12.92 Author

The knapped flint station of pleasing design at Cookham. The notice below the stop board reads, 'Wait for white light and whistle before proceeding'. This refers to the crossing beyond.

29.12.92 Author

The former 'Down' platform at Cookham now given over to non-railway use. The building has been extended.

29.12.92 Author

Twyford to Wargrave

A bill for building a branch from Twyford to Henley was put forward unsuccessfully in 1846. A second attempt the following year led to an Act being passed on 27 July 1847, but the depression following the Railway Mania delayed construction and no positive action was taken until powers were revived in 1853, construction beginning in the winter of 1854–5. Work was easy except for a 230 yd long timber bridge, Shiplake viaduct, across the Thames into Oxfordshire. This structure was subject to a 20 mph speed restriction. The single broad gauge line opened on 1 June 1857 with a public breakfast at Henley Town Hall. The five trains each way connected at Twyford with 'Up' rather than 'Down' trains, so were not convenient to those passengers going west. As no reduced fares were available from Henley, some people going to London travelled to Reading by coach in order to avail themselves of cheap tickets.

The branch was converted to standard gauge in 1876, the penultimate solely broad gauge branch east of Bristol to be converted. Work started at 9.30 p.m. on 31 March and was completed in twelve hours. In 1878 a siding was put in to serve Davis' flour mill at Tywford, which had replaced a silk mill. This siding remained in use until the 1950s.

Twyford station was rebuilt when the main line was quadrupled in the 1890s. The Henley branch made a junction with the Relief line and the bay platform was situated at the 'Down' end of the 'Up' Relief platform. Nearby was a goods shed, coal wharves, cattle pens and a gas tank wagon siding.

Henley developed as a popular holiday resort and dormitory town, and business during the summer was often brisk. To cope with this traffic, in 1897 the track was doubled and the junction at Twyford improved to give through running to and from Paddington. It was also planned to extend the Bourne End to Marlow branch to link with the existing line at Henley, but this scheme was successfully opposed by rowing clubs.

The branch was singled in June 1961, except for the Twyford end, while the East and West signal-boxes at Twyford closed on 23 October 1961 and were replaced by a new box between the 'Down' Henley branch line and the 'Up' Relief. It had a short life, as from 20 March 1972 Reading panel box controlled the branch. At Twyford the double-track junction was singled on 11 March 1972, all trains using the former 'Up' line. On the same date, a new crossover just east of the station was brought into use so that trains from the 'Down' Relief could gain access to the branch via the 'Up' Relief platform.

When the branch opened, the only intermediate station between Twyford and Henley was at Shiplake, but a station with two 500 ft long platforms opened at Wargrave on 1 October 1900. On the 'Up' side was a large standard GWR red-brick building, relieved by blue lintels. In 1946 cycle storage accommodation was provided at a cost of £110. Twyford and Wargrave both closed to goods on 7 September 1964, Wargrave being partly unstaffed from 31 January 1965.

The branch helped Henley Regatta to become more popular as it eased access. Extra staff were needed to cope with the traffic and as lodgings were difficult to find at this busy period, the GWR stabled a dining saloon and coach there to accommodate its staff. During the 1912 Regatta week passengers returning from Henley to London after the Phyllis Court Ball had a special at 2.30 a.m. on which soup and poached eggs were served. The Regatta traffic declined after the Second World War.

The branch pioneered Automatic Train Control when in January 1906 audible distant signals were introduced. The apparatus consisted of a ramp formed by an insulated steel bar on a baulk of timber laid centrally between the rails and a spring contact shoe under the engine so fixed as to be raised 1½ in when passing over the ramp. If the distant signal was at All Clear, the ramp was electrified and the current passing through the shoe rang a bell in the engine cab, but if the signal was at Caution, or any failure occurred, the ramp remained electrically dead and the raising of the shoe broke a local circuit on the engine and thereby caused a steam whistle to blow in the cab until silenced by the driver.

In 1902, out of a total of nineteen trains, three ran from the branch through to Paddington and five returned, one being a slip coach off the 9.15 p.m. 'South Wales Mail', while on Saturdays a further slip coach was provided from the 12.15 a.m. 'Fast Corridor' Paddington to Liverpool, enabling passengers to arrive at Henley at 1.20 a.m. Around 1911 the branch train consisted of two six-wheel composite coaches and two bogie brake-thirds. Today the branch has a service of twenty-two trains each way.

All engines were allowed over the branch except the heavier 2–6–2Ts, 'Castles' and 'Kings', and later all except the latter were permitted. The fast trains to and from Paddington were 4–6–0-hauled, while steam railcars and later auto-trains were used for the shuttle to Reading. The branch engine, a Metro 2–4–0T in the early days and a 57XX or 8750 class 0–6–0PT later, was kept in the shed at Henley. In October 1958 the branch was dieselized but through trains to Paddington were still steam-hauled until June 1963. However, 1958 was not the first time the branch had seen a diesel railcar, as the GWR variety had put in an appearance as early as 1934.

On Sundays in November 1992, the Severn Valley Railway's preserved class 2MT 2–6–0 No. 46251 worked shuttle trains between Twyford and Henley, BR not running a Sunday service on the branch during the winter. As there is no run-round facility, a class 37 diesel-electric was coupled to the rear of the five-coach train to work it back to Twyford.

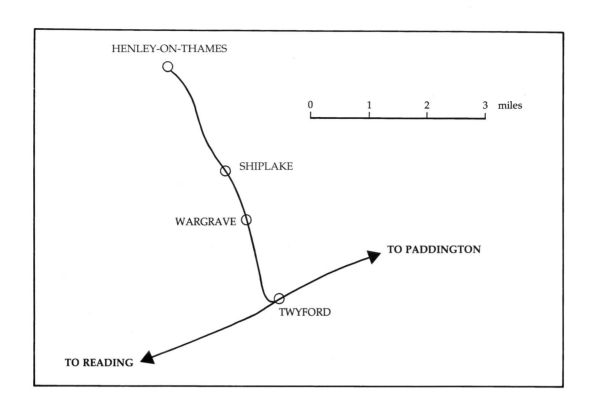

HENLEY-ON-THAMES

SHIPLAKE

WARGRAVE

TO PADDINGTON

TWYFORD

TO READING

0   1   2   3   miles

The original two-track Twyford station. The crossbar indicates 'danger' to the 'Down' train. On the far left is the Henley branch bay platform. In the centre is the goods shed, while to the right of the main building, Simonds' ales are advertised on an end wall. The artist has mis-spelt the name.

c. 1852 George Measom

View east at Twyford after quadrupling, with the signal-box standing between the Main and Relief roads. On the far left a tank engine with a very full bunker heads a passenger train at the branch platform.

Paul Strong collection

A 2221 class 4–4–2T 'County Tank' heads a stopping train, perhaps from Henley, at the 'Up' Relief platform, Twyford. Notice the shrubs on the embankment and the neatly-kept platforms.

c. 1907 Lens of Sutton

61XX class 2–6–2T No. 6106 (preserved by the Great Western Society) with a bogie van takes the Henley branch line from the 'Down' Relief en route for display at the Henley Festival. The new signal-box stands in the background.

24.6.67 S.P.J.A. Derek

View towards Henley, with the main lines behind the photographer. Twyford signal-box opened on 23 October 1961 and closed on 11 March 1972 when the double-track junction was singled.

23.6.71 Derrick Payne

Wargrave station, looking in the 'Down' direction.

c. 1905 Author's collection

An 0–4–2T heads an 'Up' auto-trailer at Wargrave. Note the concrete sleepers in the 6 ft way await-ing laying. On the right of the engine are two corrugated-iron lock-up huts.

1952 Frank J. Saunders

Wargrave station after the line had been singled. The foot-bridge and lock-ups have been removed, the seat is at an angle, paving stones are cracked and the station has an air of neglect. Commuters' vehicles crowd the car-park.

23.6.71 Derrick Payne

Wargrave station, looking in the 'Up' direction.

23.6.71 Derrick Payne

Reading to Mortimer

In 1844 the Berks and Hants Railway was proposed to run from the GWR at Reading to Basingstoke. The London and South Western Railway countered this threat to its territory by planning a line from Basingstoke to Didcot. However, the GWR won the day and the Berks and Hants was authorized on 30 June 1845, I.K. Brunel being the line's engineer. The construction was let in one contract and basically finished in August 1847, the final completion being delayed by the LSWR's awkwardness.

On 1 November 1848 the 15½ miles of broad gauge line between Reading and Basingstoke opened, giving through communication between north and south without the necessity of travelling via London, though, due to the break of gauge, through trains could not be run until 22 December 1856 when the branch was converted to mixed gauge.

The Basingstoke branch actually began at Southcote Junction, named after a nearby manor house, just under 2 miles from Reading station, the line between the GWR and Southcote Junction being shared by BHR trains to Newbury and Hungerford. Mortimer was the only intermediate station on the Basingstoke branch, though Bramley, formerly only a goods siding, was opened as a passenger station in April 1895. Brunel's Italianate building at Mortimer in red and yellow brick used the device of a hipped roof which was too large for its building and extended forward as a canopy. The Duke of Wellington, as an important landowner, had a clause inserted in the BHR Act forbidding the opening without his consent of any station within 5 miles of his seat at Stratfield Saye. When his neighbours asked for a station to be provided at Stratfield Mortimer, only 2 miles distant, he agreed, the railway promising that the building would be 'as commodious as His Grace may think fit to require'. The 'commodious' edifice is on the 'Up' side, matched by a small shelter on the 'Down' platform. It is now a Grade II listed building.

From 1937 the Lambourn Valley AEC diesel railcar No. 18 made its first run of the day from Reading to Basingstoke with the Royal Mail before returning to Reading for its run to Newbury and the LVR.

As well as being used by Reading to Basingstoke local traffic, the branch has long been important as a through route. On 1 July 1902 a Newcastle to Bournemouth through service was inaugurated using Great Central Railway stock. In 1939 two of the eighteen trains which ran over the branch daily originated north of Oxford. In 1959 Eastern Region B1 class 4-6-0s from the ex-GCR line ran through to Oxford, Reading West and Basingstoke en route to the SR. In 1962 the local service from Reading to Basingstoke was dieselized using the relatively rare three-car Berkshire DEMUs with above-floor mounted engines and two traction motors on the inner bogies. Thirty-one years later these units are still operating the service and on the Basingstoke line carry the route code 66.

Presently on Monday to Friday there are forty-four trains each way daily, including:

3 Reading–Salisbury
1 Derby–Bournemouth
2 Manchester Piccadilly–Bournemouth
1 Newcastle-upon-Tyne–Bournemouth
The 'Wessex Scot', Edinburgh–Poole
1 Leeds–Poole
1 Manchester Piccadilly–Poole
1 Liverpool–Poole.

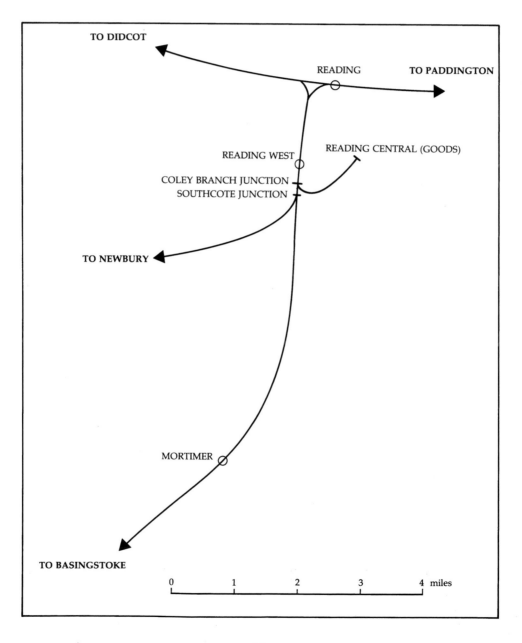

'Reading Junction for Newbury & Devizes Line & Basingstoke Branch' reads the board on the left. 'Bulldog' class 4–4–0 No. 3351 *Sedgemoor* stands at the 'Down' Relief platform with a special train. Notice the decorated headboard and lamps. The engine has been well cleaned and its buffers burnished.

c. 1907 Author's collection

The Italianate main frontage of Reading GWR station built in 1868. The central clock tower is surmounted by a finial, an enlarged copy of those used on contemporary semaphore signals. At the time of its construction it was the tallest building in the vicinity, but today is dwarfed by tower blocks.

c. 1915 Author's collection

The 10.30 a.m. Poole to Newcastle-upon-Tyne, headed by class 5 4–6–0 No. 44942, joins the Paddington to Bristol main line at Reading West Junction.

13.7.66 S.P.J.A. Derek

The 8.30 a.m. Newcastle-upon-Tyne to Poole on the curve between Reading West Junction and Oxford Road Junction behind 'West Country' class Pacific No. 34005 *Barnstaple*. This was the last day of steam on this service before the closure of the former Great Central Railway's main line.

3.9.66 S.P.J.A. Derek

The 10.30 a.m. Poole to Newcastle-upon-Tyne, headed by class 5 4–6–0 No. 44780, diverges from the main West of England line at Oxford Road Junction after calling at Reading West (the foot-bridge and platform are visible) and heads towards Reading West Junction.

26.5.66 S.P.J.A. Derek

A group of railwaymen, including a shunter with his pole, stand on the 'Up' platform at Mortimer. On the right is an unusually large station garden laid out in formal style; today it is a car-park. A small horse-bus and horse and trap stand in the station yard. The track is on longitudinal sleepers and the narrowing of the gauge gives plenty of room between the two tracks for the ganger and his mate to stand. In the mist beyond the station is the goods shed and about twenty-five wagons and vans.

c. 1904 Author's collection

The view looking the opposite way towards the overbridge from which the previous view was taken. The large overhanging eaves forming a canopy over the platform are easily visible in this view of a typical Brunelian country station. The bridge abutment has been whitened to give better sighting of the signal. The advertisement on the end wall of the main station building is for the Phoenix Fire Office. An open wagon stands in the loading dock on the far left.

Card postmarked 25.8.04 Paul Strong collection

In this early 1960s view, a covered foot-bridge has been erected to avoid passengers having to use the roadbridge. The 'Up' track has been relaid with flat-bottomed rail on timber sleepers. The points in the right foreground lead to the goods shed. Weeds grow in the cracks of the paving stones. The Southern Region, which had taken over the line, has replaced the GWR 'Down' starting signal with an upper quadrant type and positioned it on the left-hand side of the line, the brick-work being painted white behind it.

c. 1960 Lens of Sutton

In this contemporary view taken on a frosty morning, the goods sidings have been lifted, the covered foot-bridge replaced by one of the open variety and the upper quadrant signal replaced by a colour light, the white brickwork behind now looking decidedly grubby. The original slated roof has been replaced by tiles, giving the structure a heavier and less pleasant appearance.

29.12.92 Author

A close-up of the main station building at Mortimer.

29.12.92 Author

DEMU set 207 017, comprising cars Nos 60142, 60616 and 60916, stands at Mortimer with the 0918 Reading to Basingstoke service. Compare this with the lower picture on page 38.

29.12.92 Author

4–6–0 No. 6851 *Hurst Grange* with a Bournemouth to Birmingham Snow Hill train near Mortimer. The ten-coach SR set is No. 274.

6.8.55 Frank J. Saunders

'King Arthur' class 4–6–0 No. 30773 *Sir Lavaine* passing through Mortimer with a Newcastle-upon-Tyne to Bournemouth train comprising SR coaches. The SR replacement upper quadrant starting signal has a GWR-type finial. The notice at the end of the platform discourages passengers from using the barrow crossing and announces: 'Passengers are requested to cross the line by the bridge.'

30.7.60 Frank J. Saunders

Southcote Junction to Reading Central
(The Coley Branch)

In order to reduce the amount of cartage work due to the position of Reading station on the north side of the town, it was decided to build a branch to a central goods depot. The 1¾ mile long line was authorized by the GWR (Additional Powers) Act of 4 August 1905 and opened on 4 May 1908. The depot itself was constructed by Henry Lovatt and Company, Wolverhampton. However, before building the yard, the GWR was required to resite a Masonic temple which stood on the land. The branch left the BHR line immediately north of Southcote Junction and much of it originally ran through rural surroundings, despite the close proximity of the town. The single line was operated on the one engine in steam principle and was freight-only, but passenger stock from football specials was stabled there. At first speed was restricted to 15 mph, but by 1945 this had been raised to 30 mph. The only GWR engines banned from the branch were the 'Kings'. As no locomotive watering facilities were provided, the train engine, usually of tender variety with a more ample supply than a tank engine, shunted the yard.

This had twelve sidings holding a total of about three hundred wagons. The sidings were arranged in pairs, each provided with its own roadway. The yard had a goods shed, offices and cranes. It handled coal, timber, brick, stone, hay, straw and fertilizer. Connection was made with various private sidings: the Co-operative Wholesale Society Company Limited's jam factory; Anglo-American Oil (later Esso); Messrs Baynes, timber merchants; and H. and G. Simonds' Brewery. The CWS operated a four-wheel petrol-mechanical engine built by F.C. Hibberd and Company Limited, works No. 2213, in 1939. However, it was withdrawn and cut up in September 1964 when all traffic switched to road. Additionally there were three sidings at Bear wharf on the River Kennet which had facilities for off-loading rail traffic on to the water and it was not unknown for a towrope to be hooked over a locomotive's coupling in order to assist a vessel upstream. The sidings were removed on 20 March 1969.

The double-tracked Coley Branch Junction was singled on 26 May 1956. Subsequently 'Up' trains from Reading Central goods depot used the 'Down' line for a few yards before gaining the correct road via a crossover. The goods depot closed on 25 July 1983 and on 20 January 1985 the connection at Coley Branch Junction was removed.

BR Standard class 4 2–6–0 No. 76058, working tender-first, diverges from the West of England main line at Coley Branch Junction at the head of the Locomotive Club of Great Britain's hundredth railtour. The headboard reads '1953–1967 South Western Suburban Rail Tour'.

5.2.67 S.P.J.A. Derek

No. 76058 runs round the LCGB special at Reading Central goods depot.

5.2.67 S.P.J.A. Derek

Reading Central goods depot. The spacious sidings have yet to be fully utilized.

c. 1908 GWR

The LCGB special passing Reading West after the visit to Reading Central goods depot. It has travelled 'wrong line' from Coley Branch Junction and is crossing to the 'Up' line. Notice the 15 mph restriction sign.

5.2.67 S.P.J.A. Derek

2251 class 0–6–0 No. 2245 at Reading Central, looking towards the depot from the yard's throat. To the right of the locomotive is a platelayer's trolley, demounted from its wheels.

3.11.56 Hugh Davies

The Railway Enthusiasts' Club 'The Compass Rose' tour at Reading Central, headed by M7 class 0–4–4T No. 30051. In this view timber is the principal traffic.

3.10.57 N.C. Simmons

Cholsey and Moulsford to Wallingford

Wallingford and Watlington were two of the towns a short distance from the GWR's main line which, with the development of railways, desired to be served by a branch. Although by December 1840 Moulsford station had been renamed Wallingford Road, this did not make Wallingford any nearer! Its inhabitants pressed for a rail link and eventually the Wallingford and Watlington Railway Act of 25 July 1864 authorized as an initial stage the construction of a 3¼ mile long line from Wallingford Road station to Wallingford. Thomas White, the contractor, found the construction relatively simple as there were no large engineering features to contend with and no intermediate stations were required. As the line traversed the floor of the Thames Valley, gradients were easy, the steepest incline being 1 in 202. It had the honour, possibly dubious, of being the first standard gauge branch from the Paddington to Bristol line.

With the opening of the branch on 2 July 1866, Wallingford Road station reverted to Moulsford. Wallingford trains used a bay platform at the west end of the 'Up' platform, and for its first three-quarters of a mile the branch ran alongside the main line. Shortage of funds caused the abandonment of the project to extend the line across the Thames to Watlington, though eventually that town was served by a branch which opened from Princes Risborough on 15 August 1872. Worked by the GWR from the outset under an agreement of 30 June 1866, the Wallingford company found itself in financial difficulties and, like so many similar short lines, was sold to the company which worked it. Under the GWR Act of 18 July 1872 that company took over the Wallingford and Watlington Railway on 2 December.

When the main line was quadrupled in 1892, Moulsford station was closed and replaced on 29 February 1892 by a new station, Cholsey and Moulsford, nearly three-quarters of a mile to the west and close to the point where the branch swung northwards from the main line. As the station was on an embankment, J. Ward Armstrong designed it as a two-storey structure with the platforms level with the upper floor. The plain façade in brick had concrete lintels with relieving arches in engineer's blue brick. The iron balusters of the staircase to the platform levels were very fine. Unusually, the actual platform, as opposed to the platform faces, were numbered, the 'Down' Fast being No. 1, the island platform for the 'Up' Fast and 'Down' Relief No. 2, and the 'Up' Relief and Branch No. 3. The main station building was adjacent to the latter platform.

Just north of Cholsey and Moulsford is an unusual double-deck bridge carrying the railway, with a footpath below, over a stream. Another interesting feature is that the branch has a section of track laid on 1930-vintage steel sleepers relaid here after use on the main line near Maidenhead. Rails on the branch are in 45 ft lengths instead of the later 60 ft standard and there is a great variety of chairs from various railways.

Wallingford station, much used by pleasure-trippers going to or from Salter's Upper Thames steamers for excursions up or down the river, had a single platform with no run-round, so when this facility was required the engine had to reverse towards the goods yard entrance. The red-brick station building was relieved with arches or lintels in light-coloured stone. The four-coach length platform edge was faced with blue and red brick. The site is now part of the Charter Way housing estate.

The goods yard had six roads, one of which served the Wallingford Gas Light and Coke Company until this traffic of five or six wagons per week ceased in 1953. The yard was provided with a cattle pen and a red-brick goods shed, made more attractive by having the wall facing the passenger platform composed of alternate courses of red and blue. To facilitate easy working, double track was extended in 1927 towards Cholsey and further lengthened in 1941. Principal goods traffic was coal, cement and grain. Outwards from Wallingford went implements from R.J. and H. Wilder, including their pitch/pile cultivators, and scrap iron from Walter Wilder. Messrs Keen built road trailers which were dispatched by rail on flat trucks. In 1925 the yard dealt with an average of forty-five goods wagons daily; annually the branch saw 7,825 milk churns and 258 cattle trucks. A little south of the goods yard a siding, opened on 1 October 1933, served the Cooperative Wholesale Society Company Limited's dairy and egg-packing station, traffic ceasing on 31 October 1962. The timber bridge over the nearby Mill Brook rested on red-brick piers.

The original Wallingford and Watlington Railway engine shed, probably built of timber, was replaced by a brick-built edifice constructed in 1890 at its rear. Each Monday a replacement locomotive was sent from Reading, but by 1933 it was supplied by Didcot. The shed was staffed by two drivers, two firemen and an overnight cleaner. Water was raised from a well immediately behind the station platform by means of a three-cylinder water pump, the small stationary steam engine being powered by steam supplied by the branch locomotive. This pump was later operated by electric power. Following the shed's closure on 11 February 1956, a locomotive was sent daily from Didcot.

It was the 0–4–2Ts which proved the most efficient and economic engines for the branch: those of the 517 class in earlier days, and the 48XX class from the mid-1930s. At least one 'Dean Goods' and ex-Midland and South Western Junction Railway 2–4–0 No. 1336 have worked over the branch, but until later years tender engines were extremely rare. Latterly, 2251 class 0–6–0s and various 0–6–0PTs worked the line. Tender engines were not generally used on the branch passenger trains; continually coupling and uncoupling the coach at termini would have been tedious and time-consuming. Locomotives generally worked chimney-first to Cholsey hauling the auto-trailer and pushing it on the return journey. Some trains were 'mixed', the limit being set at ten loaded wagons to Wallingford. The coach was stabled overnight at Wallingford.

The intensive passenger service – eighteen trains each way in 1938 – and the need to shunt the goods yard, left little time to take on water and coal. Although a coal stage was provided, coal was usually taken direct from a wagon to the bunker in order to save effort. As it was not permitted to take the auto-coach into the goods yard, the auto-train gear, which could not be readily uncoupled and recoupled, was not always connected, which meant that when proceeding to Wallingford, the fireman unofficially drove the engine from the footplate, the driver operating the brake from his position in the control vestibule of the auto-coach. Trains on the branch were subject to a limit of 30 mph. The only train on Sundays collected the milk tank from the creamery, the locomotive having to be steamed for this duty alone.

On at least one occasion, the auto-train failed to stop at Wallingford and the coach ended up outside on the A4130. The district inspector proposed sending for a pair of cranes to lift them back, but it had to be pointed out to him that the cranes' weight banned them from the branch. The coach and engine were simply drawn back.

The timetable offered six trains each way in 1889, thirteen in 1910 and eleven in 1957, but all passenger services were withdrawn on 15 June 1959, the last train consisting of six coaches, including auto-coach No. 174 built in 1930. The signal-box at Wallingford, worked by the leading porter who doubled as a signalman, closed on 19 January 1964 and the branch closed to general goods traffic on 13 September 1965. The line was then closed north of the Associated British Maltsters (Southern) Limited's mill. This siding close to the 2¼ milepost had been brought into use as recently as 13 July 1961. When in 1981 the points at Cholsey needed replacing, the cost was not considered economic, so ABM changed to road transport. The very last BR train, a six-car DMU, ran on 31 May 1981.

Although regular passenger services had been withdrawn in 1959, this was by no means the end, as on 17 June 1967 special trains ran on the day of the Wallingford Carnival, operated by the Great Western Society's 0–4–2T No. 1466 and auto-coach No. 231. The following year these services were run on two days.

On 31 May 1981, the day of the last train, sixteen-year-old Philip Garvey founded the Cholsey and Wallingford Railway Preservation Society which, with the aid of loans and the local council, has purchased the track and runs passenger services at summer weekends, and Santa Specials in December. A new platform has been erected at Wallingford. The society's logo is a cunning adaptation of the GWR's 1930s 'shirt button' design, altered to read 'C&WR'.

Locomotives Preserved on the Cholsey and Wallingford Railway

Number and name	Wheel arrangement	Builder	Works No.	Date of construction
4247	2–8–0T	GWR	2632	1916
Thames	0–4–0ST	Barclay	2351	1951
Carpenter	0–4–0D	F.C. Hibberd	3271	1949
D3190 later 08 1123, *George Mason*	0–6–0D	BR	–	1955
Iris	0–4–0D	Ruston and Hornsby	304470	1964

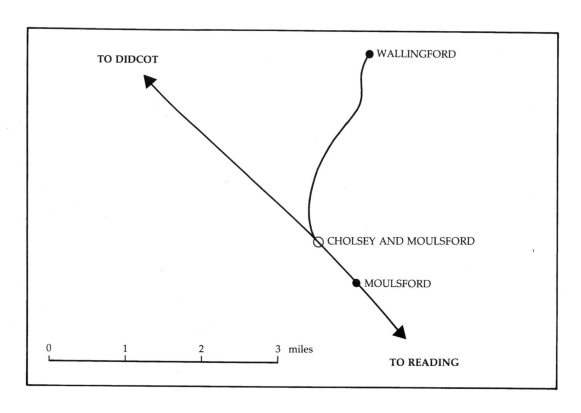

TO DIDCOT

WALLINGFORD

CHOLSEY AND MOULSFORD

MOULSFORD

0   1   2   3 miles

TO READING

CHOLSEY AND MOULSFORD
CHANCE FOR WALLINGFORD

4–6–0 No. 6996 *Blackwell Hall*, shedded at 81E (Didcot), at Cholsey and Moulsford with the 12.45 p.m. Paddington to Oxford.

6.6.59 Hugh Ballantyne

Cholsey and Moulsford. The view down the Relief lines showing the large signal-box opened on 23 July 1905 to replace the East and West signal-boxes. It closed on 9 May 1965 with the introduction of colour light signalling. Wallingford trains used a bay platform on the right at the far end of the station building.

14.6.19 Paul Strong collection

An out-of-sight 'Hymek' propels Great Western Society stock, including No. 6998 *Burton Agnes Hall*, on the Wallingford branch at Cholsey and Moulsford for a special display in connection with the Wallingford Carnival. The auto-coach is No. W231.

15.6.68 S.P.J.A. Derek

14XX class 0–4–2T No. 1407 and auto-trailer No. W174W at Wallingford with the 2.55 p.m. Saturdays-only to Cholsey and Moulsford. Dominating the scene is a conical-type water tank.

6.6.59 Hugh Ballantyne

2251 class 0–6–0 No. 3210 of 81E Didcot shed stands at Wallingford with the 5.20 p.m. to Cholsey. The double corrugated-iron shed at the far end of the platform was for cycles. The brick-built engine shed seen between the locomotive and water tank closed on 11 February 1956.

7.6.58 E. Wilmshurst

Dereliction after the withdrawal of the passenger service. The water tower has been removed from the base on the left. The corrugated-iron shed immediately to the right of the former locomotive shed was the locomotive department's oil store, separate from the main building for safety reasons.

c. 1964 Lens of Sutton

The mayor and onlookers don't appear to be sad on the last day of passenger services at Wallingford. The auto-coach on the left has a good shine. Note the nonslip bricks on the platform.

13.6.59 John Attwell Collection

The 'Wallingford Wake' special at Wallingford. DMU L435 consisted of class 117 and 118 cars Nos W51373, W59480 and W51415. Note the grain wagons standing in the Associated British Maltsters' siding.

31.5.81 Cholsey and Wallingford Railway Preservation Society

Barclay 0–4–0ST *Thames* breaking the tape on leaving the temporary Wallingford platform. GWR 20 ton brake van No. 17428, built at Swindon in 1940 and standing on the left, has been branded 'Wallingford', though being a vacuum-fitted vehicle, in GWR days it would normally have been kept for express goods duty and an ordinary hand brake van used on the branch.

17.6.90 P. Warrington

Didcot to Newbury

The story of the Didcot to Newbury line really began in 1846, the year of the Railway Mania, when many north to south routes were projected, one being the grand-sounding Oxford, Southampton, Gosport and Portsmouth Railway, which was really a 35 mile long line from the GWR at Didcot to the LSWR near Micheldever. Although this particular plan failed, the idea was not entirely shelved, and was resurrected in 1873 as the Didcot, Newbury and Southampton Railway. Unfortunately, insufficient financial support was given by local landowners and other wealthy people. In 1879, as the bill for abandonment was passing through the House of Lords, it was suddenly announced that the bill had been withdrawn – landowners had at last seen the value of the line opening up markets.

The board of directors included eminent men. Its chairman was Col. Sir Robert Loyd-Lindsay VC, of Lockinge House near Wantage, a soldier who had distinguished himself in the Crimean War. Later he became Lord Wantage. Other important directors were John Walter, MP for Berkshire and chief proprietor of *The Times*; W.G. Mount, MP for Newbury, and Sir Julius Vogel, later to become prime minister of New Zealand. John Fowler was the engineer and Messrs Falkiner and Tancred the contractors, the trio responsible a few years later for building the Forth Bridge. John Fowler made some alterations to the Didcot, Newbury and Southampton Railway, the chief one being at Newbury where the GWR station was utilized instead of having an independent line with no connection to the GWR.

On 26 August 1879 the first sod was ceremonially turned by Lady Carnarvon in a field at Newbury between Woodspeen Terrace and Beaconsfield Terrace. The contractors were innovators and it is believed that they were the first in Britain to employ a steam navvy to excavate cuttings. Although the line crossed the Berkshire Downs at a height of 379 ft above sea level, the gradient nowhere exceeded 1 in 106. Although Fowler anticipated speeds of 60 mph and more, the GWR later imposed a limit of 50 mph between Didcot and Newbury.

On 28 July 1881 the directors enjoyed a trip over part of the line in a first class saloon, while the press were accommodated in a second class coach. Motive power was provided by one of the contractor's engines, appropriately named *Newbury*. The original track was flat-bottomed instead of the more usual bull-head type, and some of this original rail lasted in sidings until the line's closure.

As was the case with most small railways, it was more economical for the DNSR to be worked by a larger company than to provide its own locomotives and rolling stock. The GWR supplied thirty saloons for the two specials at the formal opening on 12 April 1882 by Lady Loyd-Lindsay, wife of the chairman, the public service beginning the next day.

In the event, instead of the southern half of the DNSR making a junction with the LSWR at Micheldever, this was effected at Shawford, south of Winchester, the DNSR being opened throughout on 1 October 1891.

During the First World War the line proved a vital link because Winchester was one of the main assembly areas for troops awaiting transport to France. Passenger services on the DNSR were suspended for periods from August to October 1914 in order to make paths for these troop specials.

In 1923 the DNSR was absorbed by the GWR. In the Second World War the line again became a major artery and, in preparation for the Normandy Landings in 1944, from August 1942 all passenger services and day goods trains were suspended for eight months in order for the line to be doubled. This operation was made easier by the fact that when the line was built, earthworks and bridges were made wide enough for two tracks. As many as 16,000 military trains used the line in the twelve months leading up to D-Day. Passenger services over the line were withdrawn on 10 September 1962 and freight on 10 August 1964, the track being lifted three years later.

A great variety of GWR locomotives worked over the line. A GWR diesel railcar made a trial run on 30 April 1947 but the experiment was not repeated. In March 1955 Southern Region Class T9 4–4–0s began regular working over the line, while between 1957 and 1959 No. 3440 *City of Truro*, of 102 mph fame, taken out of retirement to earn her keep on enthusiasts' trains after being in York Railway Museum for twenty-six years, was shedded at Didcot, and between specials worked trains to Southampton. Latterly, BR Standard class 9F 2–10–0s worked oil trains over the line to and from Fawley, while the last passenger trains between Didcot and Newbury were worked by DMUs.

The first station on the branch, Upton and Blewbury, was called Upton until 16 January 1911. Like most of the other DNSR stations, it was a delightful red-brick and tiled building, more like a Victorian villa than a station. It had dormer windows, decorated bargeboards, and its canopy, supported on wooden columns, was tiled, this latter being quite an unusual feature. On the opposite platform stood a simple timber shelter. The goods shed, like most of those on the DNSR, was a small building beside the track, rather than a large one spanning it. The area was, and still is, training country for racehorses, 229 being dealt with at the station in 1909. They were loaded from the passenger platform as no special facilities were provided until the following year.

Churn station was built because Lord Wantage, a DNSR director and a member of the National Rifle Association, invited the association to meet on Churn Down to assess the suitability of the site for the annual competition; a platform was ready on 6 July 1888 for visitors to the event. Although the NRA found the location unsuitable and two years later used Bisley, summer camps for volunteer regiments were held annually at Churn, so the company's outlay was not wasted. The army held its summer camps near the station and two thousand men, plus horses and mules, depended on the railway for transport and supplies. When the line was doubled, Churn became an island platform, acting as a public platform from May 1905, but with the stipulation that 'evening trains call during the hours of daylight only'. This was because the platform was unlit and over half a mile from the nearest road.

Compton was the most important station on the section and the only one on the DNSR, apart from Winchester, to boast a foot-bridge. It also had a much larger goods shed than the standard DNSR pattern, and wagons could be unloaded and loaded under cover. Its horse-loading bank dealt with a considerable number of racehorses in the days before these animals were transported by road. Hampstead Norris had a single-storey station building and no crossing loop, while Pinewood Halt opened on 11 September 1933 to attract passengers from the northern end of the village of Hermitage. Near the halt a spur led to Brain's brickworks.

Hermitage was a typical DNSR station like Upton, and also had a horse-loading bank. Wagons of sand, gravel and tarmac for Berkshire County Council arrived by rail. As the tar was in open wagons it was difficult to unload in cold weather and when a council steamroller was unavailable to provide heat for this operation, fires were lit under the wagons. South of the station were the National Cold Store sidings.

Newbury station, built by the Berks and Hants Railway, originally had an overall roof but was rebuilt between 1908 and 1910, bay platforms being provided for terminating DNSR trains.

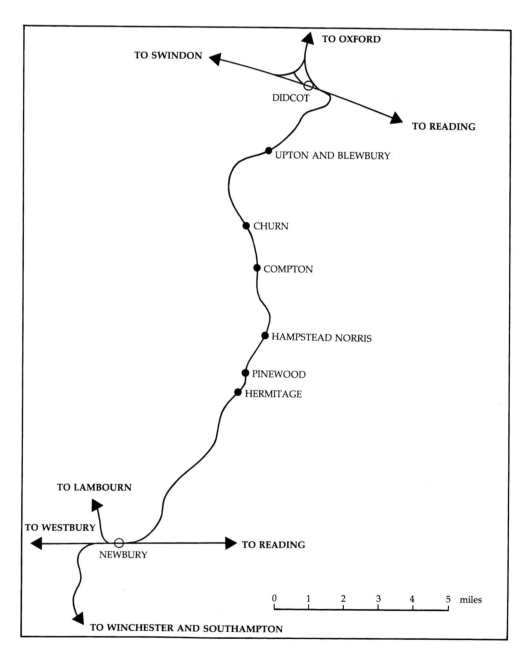

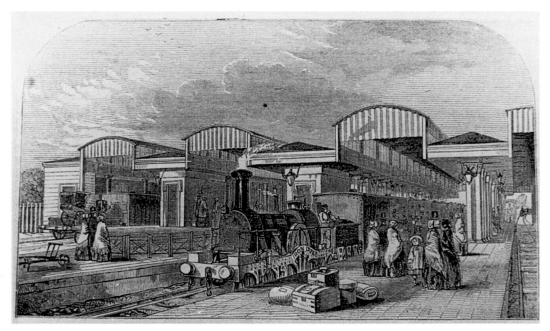

The broad gauge 4–2–2 *Iron Duke* heading a train at Didcot.

c. 1852 George Measom

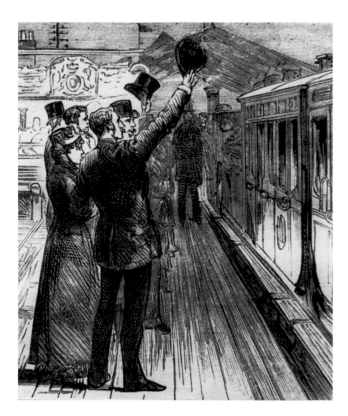

The arrival of the first Didcot, Newbury and Southampton Railway train at Didcot.
12.4.1882 *The Graphic*

Salute of anvils on the opening day of the DNSR.
12.4.1882 *The Graphic*

The DNSR opening ceremony at London Road bridge, just outside Newbury.

12.4.1882 *The Graphic*

Racehorses on a training ground near Compton being frightened by a passing train.

12.4.1882 *The Graphic*

Newbury *en fête* at the opening of the DNSR.

12.4.1882 *The Graphic*

4–4–0 No. 3440 *City of Truro* at Didcot in the late 1950s with a train to Southampton.

Paul Strong collection

2251 class 0–6–0 No. 2214 at the isolated Churn station with an 'Up' train. An island platform at a wayside GWR station was unusual but not unique.

c. 1958 Lens of Sutton

2251 class 0–6–0 No. 2246 passing the attractive signal-box at Compton with the 10.50 a.m. Didcot to Newbury composed of Southern Region coaching stock.

5.7.58 E. Wilmshurst

Ex-LSWR T9 class 4–4–0 No. 30117 leaves Compton with a 'Down' train. The concrete foot-bridge is an unusual structure built in the 1950s. It was provided for a public right of way which crossed the line and connected the village with the church.

c. 1958 Lens of Sutton

Compton station name board and signal-box plates preserved at the Didcot Railway Centre.

19.8.92 Author

Ex-LSWR T9 class 4–4–0 No. 30301 at Hampstead Norris with a Southampton to Didcot train. There was only a single platform here until the line was doubled during the Second World War. The new concrete 'Down' platform can be seen on the left.

9.4.59 Author's collection

British Railways Standard class 9F 2–10–0 No. 92211 makes a contrast of locomotive power with the previous plate. It is passing Pinewood Halt with the 9.50 a.m. Didcot to Eastleigh goods.

16.12.61 E. Wilmshurst

2251 class 0–6–0 No. 3212 passing Pinewood Halt with an 'Up' goods.

c. 1960 Lens of Sutton

A single-car DMU at Hermitage working the 10.50 a.m. Didcot to Newbury. Accommodation problems at the station were eased in the 1920s with the provision of a wooden parcels shed at the far end of the building.

16.12.61 E. Wilmshurst

A 2–4–0 heads a stopping train at Newbury. This picture was taken before the train shed was demolished in the 1908–10 station rebuilding.

c. 1904 Author's collection

Interior of the goods shed at Newbury, showing the hand crane and the wide variety of consign-
ments it loaded and unloaded. Boxes of Sunlight soap are on the cart to the right, destined for a
local grocer's shop. The wagon behind the men has a rail to support the tarpaulin so that any rain
would run off.

c. 1905 Author's collection

No. 6025 *King Henry III* passes Enborne Junction, west of Newbury, with the 8.30 a.m.
Plymouth–Paddington express. The DNSR to Woodhay and Winchester curves to the left.

1.8.55 Author's collection

SUSPENSION OF PASSENGER TRAIN SERVICE

BETWEEN

DIDCOT, NEWBURY

AND

WINCHESTER (Cheesehill)

(GWR)

NOTICE IS HEREBY GIVEN THAT OWING TO ENGINEERING WORK THE

PASSENGER TRAIN SERVICE

BETWEEN DIDCOT, NEWBURY and WINCHESTER (Cheesehill)

WILL BE SUSPENDED ON

TUESDAY, AUGUST 4th, 1942

AND UNTIL FURTHER NOTICE.

The 11.30 p.m. (Week Days) Winchester (Cheesehill) to Sutton Scotney will continue to run for the present, but will be subject to cancellation at short notice.

A ROAD SERVICE for the conveyance of passengers only and WITH STRICTLY LIMITED ACCOMMODATION will be provided in lieu of the rail service, as under. This service will be subject to alteration or cancellation at short notice, and the Great Western Railway Company and the Omnibus Companies operating on their behalf CANNOT GUARANTEE ACCOMMODATION BY ANY PARTICULAR SERVICE.

DIDCOT TO NEWBURY AND NEWBURY TO WINCHESTER (Cheesehill)

STATIONS		a.m.	a.m.	a.m.	a.m.	p.m.	p.m.	p.m.	p.m.	p.m.	p.m.	p.m.	p.m.	Suns. p.m.	Suns. p.m.
DIDCOT	dep.	..	..	7 30	..	..	12 15	..	3 15	..	5 52	6 30	..	3 35	3 0
Upton & Blewbury	"	..	..	7 41	..	..	12 26	..	3 26	..	6 3	—	..	3 46	3 8
Churn	"	..	..	8 5	..	..	12 50	..	—	..	6 17	—	..	—	—
Compton	"	..	..	8 15	..	..	1 0	..	3 36	..	6 27	—	..	3 56	3 21
Hampstead Norris	"	..	..	8 25	..	..	1 10	..	3 46	..	6 37	—	..	9 6	3 27
Pinewood Halt	"	..	..	8 30	..	..	1 15	..	3 51	..	6 42	—	..	9 11	3 33
Hermitage	"	..	..	8 36	..	..	1 21	..	3 57	..	6 48	—	..	9 17	3 37
NEWBURY	arr.	..	..	8 52	..	..	1 37	..	4 13	..	7 4	7 20	..	9 33	3 45
NEWBURY	dep.	5 20	7 45	..	9 5	12 35	..	2 5	..	4 30	..	..	7 25		..
Woodhay	"	5 29	7 54	..	9 14	12 44	..	2 14	..	4 39	..	..	7 34		..
Highclere	"	5 41	8 6	..	9 26	12 56	..	2 26	..	4 51	..	..	7 46		..
Burghclere	"	5 50	8 15	..	9 35	1 5	..	2 35	..	5 0	..	..	7 55	Saturdays excepted	..
Litchfield	"	6 2	8 27	..	9 47	1 17	..	2 47	..	5 12	..	..	8 7		..
Whitchurch	"	6 14	8 39	..	9 59	1 29	..	2 59	..	5 24	..	..	8 19		..
Sutton Scotney	"	6 32	8 57	..	10 17	1 47	..	3 17	..	5 42	..	..	8 37		..
Worthy Down Platform	"	6 44	9 9	..	10 29	1 59	..	3 29	..	5 54	..	..	8 49		..
King's Worthy	"	6 53	9 18	..	10 38	2 8	..	3 38	..	6 3	..	..	8 58		..
WINCHESTER (Cheesehill)	arr.	6 59	9 24	..	10 44	2 14	..	3 44	..	6 9	..	..	9 4		..

WINCHESTER (Cheesehill) TO NEWBURY AND NEWBURY TO DIDCOT

STATIONS		a.m.	a.m.	a.m.	a.m.	noon	p.m.	p.m.	p.m.	p.m.	p.m.	p.m.	p.m.	Suns. p.m.
WINCHESTER (Cheesehill)	dep.	..	7 5	..	9 35	12 0	..	2 42	..	5 33	..	6 15	9 10	..
King's Worthy	"	..	7 11	..	9 41	12 6	..	2 47	..	5 39	..	6 21	9 16	..
Worthy Down Platform	"	..	7 20	..	9 50	12 15	..	2 55	..	5 48	..	6 30	9 25	..
Sutton Scotney	"	..	7 32	..	10 2	12 27	..	3 6	..	6 0	..	6 42	9 37	..
Whitchurch	"	..	7 50	..	10 20	12 45	..	3 13	..	6 18	..	7 0	9 55	..
Litchfield	"	..	8 2	..	10 32	12 57	..	3 24	..	6 30	..	7 12	10 7	..
Burghclere	"	..	8 14	..	10 44	1 9	..	3 35	..	6 42	..	7 24	10 19	..
Highclere	"	..	8 23	..	10 53	1 18	..	3 43	..	6 51	..	7 33	10 28	..
Woodhay	"	..	8 35	..	11 5	1 30	..	3 54	..	7 3	..	7 45	10 40	..
NEWBURY	arr.	..	8 44	..	11 14	1 39	..	4 12	..	7 12	..	7 54	10 49	..
NEWBURY	dep.	6 30	..	9 15	..	..	1 50	..	4 15	..	7 15	..	..	8 10
Hermitage	"	6 46	..	9 31	..	..	2 6	..	4 31	..	7 31	..	..	8 20
Pinewood Halt	"	6 52	..	9 37	..	..	2 12	..	4 37	..	7 37	..	..	8 24
Hampstead Norris	"	6 57	..	9 42	..	..	2 17	..	4 42	..	7 42	..	..	8 32
Compton	"	7 7	..	9 52	..	..	2 27	..	4 52	..	7 52	..	..	8 40
Churn	"	—	..	10 2	..	..	2 37	..	—	..	8 2	..	..	..
Upton & Blewbury	"	7 17	..	10 26	..	..	3 1	..	5 2	..	8 26	..	..	8 52
DIDCOT	arr.	7 28	..	10 37	..	..	3 12	..	5 13	..	8 37	..	..	9 0

PASSENGERS WILL BE PICKED UP AND SET DOWN AT THE STATIONS AND HALTS SHEWN ABOVE.
TICKETS MUST BE TAKEN AT THE STATION BOOKING OFFICES IN THE USUAL WAY.

PADDINGTON,
August, 1942.

JAMES MILNE,
General Manager.

8,800. Printed in Great Britain by WYMAN & SONS LTD., London, Reading and Fakenham.—8584.

Notice of suspension of the passenger train service between Didcot and Newbury in order that the line could be doubled.

Radley to Abingdon

Following the passing of the GWR Act in 1835, some pressed for a link to Abingdon. The scheme was placed before Parliament in 1837 and 1838, but was unsuccessful due to the opposition of the local council and Mr Duffield, MP. From 20 July 1840, when the GWR was opened as far as Steventon, Abingdon inhabitants wishing to travel by train had to reach this railhead by road. In 1844, when the Oxford and Great Western Union Railway was built, due to the interference of three influential landowners the line ran from Didcot to Oxford direct instead of via Abingdon. Had these landowners, not been against the railway, Abingdon might have retained its status as county town instead of ceding it to Reading.

The following decade the corporation had a change of heart and the Abingdon Railway from Radley was authorized by Parliament on 15 June 1855. The contractor, George Furness, built the branch rapidly and it opened on 2 June the following year. The inaugural train carried directors and shareholders from Abingdon to Warwick, the day culminating in a champagne dinner in the County Hall, Abingdon and a 'substantial' meal for 120 navvies at The Rising Sun. On this opening day Abingdon also celebrated the end of the Crimean War with bun-throwing and a vast feast in the Market Place, 7,000 lb of provisions being eaten.

The first and subsequent trains were worked by GWR 2–2–2 *Eagle*, built in 1838 by Sharp, Roberts, and replaced in the ensuing weeks by *Aeolus*, *Etna*, *Hecla* and *Vulcan*, the latter probably being the last broad gauge engine to work the branch. Opening the line caused the price of coal to drop from 25*s* to 16*s* per ton and trade at the cattle market was also boosted. An interesting feature of Abingdon Junction was that the wooden platforms on the main line enabled a passenger to change to and from the Oxford branch, but these platforms were not accessible by road. In 1873 it was replaced by a new station at Radley, three-quarters of a mile north, the branch being extended for this distance alongside the main line.

By 1865 the town council's attitude towards the railway had so changed that it even tried to entice the GWR to build a carriage and wagon works at Abingdon after Oxford City Council and the University had opposed a scheme to build a works there. Abingdon Corporation proposed that the railway use a flat area by Nuneham railway bridge and Barton Court Farm, a third of a mile east of the terminus, offering to give half the land and lend the company £20,000. However, the GWR turned down the site as it was subject to severe flooding.

The branch was changed from broad to standard gauge in just one day, 26 November 1872, conversion being relatively easy as the track had been laid on transverse sleepers, so it was just a matter of lifting one rail into a new line of chairs which had previously been fixed at standard gauge distance from the others.

In 1891 the corporation sent representatives to Paddington and successfully secured a better train service on the branch. The following year it strongly opposed the suggested abolition of Sunday trains and once again achieved a victory over the GWR.

In 1904 the local company sold the line to the GWR 'at a very advantageous rate to the Abingdon shareholders', who received £20 GWR Ordinary Stock for each £10 share, but plans made by the Abingdon Railway to extend the line to Wantage Road were dropped.

At Radley the main building, constructed of brick with limestone decorations at plinth, quoins and cornice, was on the 'Up' platform, the 'Down' platform being an island with branch trains using the outer face. The platforms were extended between May 1948 and March 1949.

The original Abingdon terminus had brick offices set at right angles to a wooden Dutch barn-type shelter over the platform. The company received many letters of complaint about its condition and was forced to take action when on 22 April 1908 a goods train crashed into stationary coaches, causing a partial collapse of the station roof and rendering the structure unsafe. Although the GWR standard plans for small stations had been in use for six years, a well-proportioned unique design was used and the train shed was replaced by a platform awning. Part of the old station was removed to the permanent way depot at Reading where it was re-erected as a store. Both old and new stations at Abingdon were unusual in the fact that instead of being fenced in order to force passengers to enter or leave via the ticket collector's gate, the platform was open to the road. In 1956 the station was decorated for the arrival of the queen to reopen the historic County Hall. The station was demolished in 1971.

Abingdon had an extensive goods yard with sidings leading to a malthouse and the gasworks, the latter being disused by 1956. Goods traffic consisted largely of barley, beer, beet, coal and pelts, in addition to that required by the town's traders and local farmers. On Mondays, which was market day, cattle were driven through the streets to the station yard. Polo ponies trained at Abingdon were loaded into horseboxes. The tannery sent a steam wagon to collect pelts from the station. In 1925 Abingdon dealt with an average of thirty-three wagons daily, and annually 2,900 milk churns and 357 cattle trucks. During the Second World War three goods trains were run daily to cope with the traffic of the RAF, army, United States Forces and the MG car works. One rather grisly traffic was empty coffins to the RAF bomber station. Around 1950 the branch dealt with 2,000 tons of freight per week.

Between 1872 and 1947 passenger trains were generally worked by an 0–4–2T of the 517 class, including No. 1473 *Fair Rosamund*, the Woodstock branch engine, while ex-Monmouthshire Railway and Canal Company 4–4–0T No. 1306 appeared at the turn of the century. The 4–4–0 No. 3446 *Goldfinch* once worked a permanent way train. Towards the end of passenger services trains consisted of a single-unit DMU. Latterly, a D63XX, 'Hymek' or class 08 diesel shunter worked the freight trains. The shed at Abingdon for stabling the branch locomotive closed on 20 March 1953. Until this date the Abingdon engine principally worked the passenger trains, freight being handled by an engine from Oxford, this latter shed eventually supplying both engines daily.

In 1956, at 6.15 a.m. a 14XX class 0–4–2T ran light from Oxford and, after picking up the auto-coach at Radley, worked a parcels-only service at Abingdon, from where the first passenger service left at 7.05 a.m. When it reached Abingdon with the 11.55 a.m., the engine ran to Oxford for servicing before working the 4.55 p.m. Abingdon to Radley and operating the rest of the service. At the end of each day the passenger service finished at Abingdon, the coach being worked empty to Radley, and the engine returning light to Oxford shed, except on Saturdays when it took the coach to Oxford. Goods trains, the 1.15 p.m. passenger Abingdon to Radley and the 1.40 p.m. return were worked by an 0–6–0PT from Oxford, and in the 1950s this was often a member of the 850 class built sixty to seventy years earlier. Following the closure of Abingdon shed an 0–4–2T, rather than an 0–6–0PT, was used on goods. Although the 0–4–2T working the goods was auto-fitted, it was not worth the trouble of coupling up the apparatus for just one trip, so the engine ran round its coach at Radley.

Push-pull working was not introduced on the branch until about 1932 and up to this date trains consisted of four four-wheel coaches. Queues formed to catch the train to attend football matches, the return fare to Oxford being 1s, reduced to 6d on Saturday evening. Some passengers travelled by train to Oxford to visit the meat market there to buy their weekend joint. On at least one occasion a hop-pickers' special ran to Abingdon. In the postwar era passenger traffic on the branch was light because competing buses were more convenient and to travel from Oxford station to the city centre meant either a dreary walk or a wait for an infrequent bus service. Had the branch junction been reversed to allow through running to Reading and Paddington, traffic may have improved as Reading had a station convenient for the town centre. It is interesting that the branch train was colloquially known as the 'Abingdon Flyer' because this was the name of the eighteenth-century coach running to and from London.

Ten passenger trains ran each way over the branch in 1887, sixteen in 1922 and eighteen in 1938, latterly 5 minutes being allowed for a one-way trip. Passenger trains were limited to a maximum speed of 40 mph.

With the decline in the number of passengers, these services ceased to be profitable and were withdrawn on 9 September 1963, the remaining goods traffic being coal, barley and cars, the latter carried on twenty Carflat wagons. After the withdrawal of the MG marque in 1980 (the last car train ran on 23 May), traffic consisted of just one coal train weekly, drawn from Oxford by a class 31. The last coal train ran on 27 March 1984 and an enthusiasts' special DMU on 30 June 1984, the branch being taken out of use the following month and used by BR for training permanent way staff.

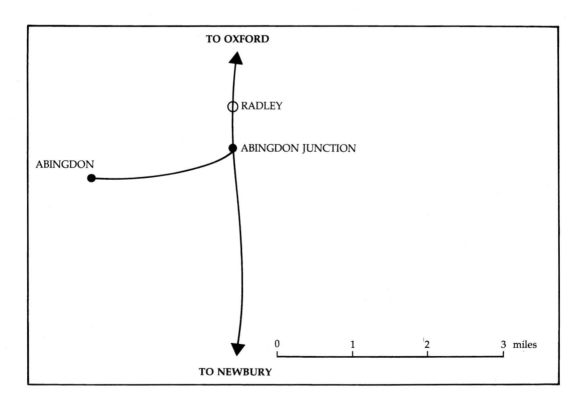

Radley. The view towards Oxford, the branch platform being on the left and the signal-box just visible on the right.

c. 1905 Author's collection

14XX class 0–4–2T No. 1435 with auto-trailer stands at the branch platform with a train for Abingdon.

7.6.58 E. Wilmshurst

Station name-plate and signal-box plate at Didcot Railway Centre.

19.8.92 Author

The LCGB 'Western Ranger' special at Radley with 28XX class 2–8–0 No. 3863 (82E, Bristol, Barrow Road), which had drawn it from Reading. 8750 class 0–6–0PT No. 9773 will take it on to Abingdon. The latter, in British Railways livery, has had its smokebox door number-plate removed and replaced with numerals on the buffer beam. Its buffers have been burnished for the occasion.

15.8.65 Hugh Ballantyne

View from the auto-trailer hauled by 58XX class 0–4–2T No. 5818 en route from Radley to Abingdon. The countryside is flat and few earthworks were required. The engine is about to pass over an occupation crossing.

c. 1958 P.Q. Treloar

517 class 0–4–2T No. 1484 at Abingdon in 1904, when this engine was allocated to Abingdon shed. Note the tool box above the tank, and the bottle-jack on the running plate. Beyond the engine is the goods shed, on the wall of which is an enamel plate advertising Sutton's seeds. The attractive gas lamp is worth a second glance.

1904 Author's collection

John North and Son's private owner's wagon No. 13 preserved at Didcot Railway Centre.

19.8.92 Author

The exterior of the original Abingdon station. Note the many advertisements and the train shed beyond.

c. 1904 Author's collection

Radley. The 'Up' view after the track had been lifted from the branch platform in the foreground. The station buildings were demolished and replaced by waiting shelters of unpleasing design.

27.6.81 Author

The new station at Abingdon with its arch portico displaying 'GWR Abingdon Station' in gilt carved wooden letters. Note the wheel stones at the corners of the building to prevent vehicles damaging the brickwork. This replacement building followed the floor plan of the original. In addition to the GWR advertisements, there are others for Maple's furniture; Van Houten's cocoa; Wood Milne shoe polish; Tower tea; Pear's soap; Stone's ginger wine; Nectar tea; Mazawattee tea; Hilton's boots; 'K' boots; Jaegar wool-lined boots and shoes; Newbury Races; New Hudson bicycles; and Alexandra oil.

c. 1912 Author's collection

Abingdon station was unusual in not being fenced off and so was completely open to the road. The platform canopy which replaced the train shed shows well in this view. The train consists of an auto-coach leading and 14XX 0–4–2T No. 1435 at its far end ready to propel to Radley.

7.6.58 E. Wilmshurst

An auto-trailer at Abingdon in the charge of 14XX class 0–4–2T No. 1435. For transferring passengers a helpful notice reads, 'To the River & Salters' steamers.'

c. 1960 Lens of Sutton

The end-loading dock at Abingdon for wheeled vehicles shows well in this view. Non-auto-fitted engines used the line on the left for running round.

c. 1960 Lens of Sutton

58XX class 0–4–2T No. 5818 at Abingdon. As this class was not auto-fitted, the engine would have had to run round the coach. Note the parcels being unloaded from the guard's compartment, and the goods shed in the background. The skylights give the platform a bright appearance. On the engine, the fireman has a spare shovel on the handrail, and a water bucket for washing and other purposes hangs on a hook beneath the bunker. The pet pipe drapes over the side of the cab. No lamp is visible, so it has probably been placed on the other end of the locomotive ready for the return journey. The top lamp bracket on the bunker has been severely bent when loading coal.

c. 1958 P.Q. Treloar

58XX class 0–4–2T No. 5818 entering Abingdon station. From left to right note the goods sidings, cattle pens in front of the goods shed, loading gauge, and signal-box of timber construction on a brick base.

c. 1958 P.Q. Treloar

Memories of the past were revived at the Abingdon Festival. A DMU working a special shuttle service for the occasion from Radley stands at the passenger platform, now devoid of its canopy. Great Western Society 14XX class 0–4–2T No. 1466 and auto-trailer No. 231 are in the foreground, while the GWS 61XX class 2–6–2T No. 6106 stands by the goods shed.

23.5.70 S.P.J.A. Derek

Abingdon station towards the end of its life; empty coal wagons await dispatch.

27.6.81 Author

Wantage Road to Wantage

The GWR's route through the Vale of the White Horse was 2½ miles distant from Wantage. In 1866 the Wantage and Great Western Railway was promoted, but failed to gain sufficient support. Following the passing of the Tramways Act of 1870, the idea was aired of laying a roadside tramway between Wantage and Wantage Road station, this being considerably cheaper than constructing a branch line. Although it was intimated that initially horses would be used, it was intended to use steam locomotives at an early date. A meeting was held at Wantage Town Hall on 22 October 1873 and £3,000 of the estimated £9,000 required was promised. Moving quickly, the Wantage Tramway Company Limited was registered on 10 November 1873 and the line authorized by Parliament on 7 August 1874. Philip Ward of Birmingham started construction in December 1874, the heaviest engineering work being the 38 ft span bridge over the Wilts and Berks Canal at Grove. The line was finished and ready for the Board of Trade inspection by Col. C.S. Hutchinson on 26 August 1875, this being carried out in a horse-drawn tramcar.

The line opened to goods on 1 October 1875 and to passengers on 11 October. As only one car was available, Nunney's horse bus, which had worked the service prior to the tramway opening, was retained until a second car was purchased in December. Nunney was paid £100 for the goodwill and his GWR parcel agency. The opening of the tramway reduced the transport cost of coal per ton from 2s 6d to 1s.

As early as 25 September 1874, the company's secretary and engineer had inspected John Grantham's fifty-four seat, double-deck steam tram which had its boiler and machinery within the car rather than on a separate chassis. As Parliament had only authorized animal traction, the steam car had to be tested at the Wantage end of the line where it ran on the company's own land away from the public highway. An order to use steam power was granted on 27 June 1876. Grantham's tram began running a public service on 1 August 1876, the line being one of the first tramways in Britain to use steam as tractive power.

Before arriving at Wantage, the steam train, built by Merryweather and Sons, had worked in London between Victoria station and Vauxhall Bridge, but difficulties were experienced firing the two vertical boilers when the car was full of passengers. Like the later electric cars on urban tramways, it could be driven from either end. This machine reduced the Wantage Tramway's operating costs from 8d to 7d per train mile. In November a tram engine, as opposed to a steam tramcar, also built by Messrs Merryweather, arrived but failed to live up to expectations and was replaced by another unsuccessful machine. March 1877 saw a Hughes and Company tram engine on trial, numbered 4. Although not powerful enough to work the goods service, it could haul a passenger trailer. In May 1878 the tramway purchased, for £350 from the London and North Western Railway, 0–4–0WT *Shannon*, built by George England and Company for the Sandy and Potton Railway, a 4 mile long line in Bedfordshire. Numbered 5, it was powerful enough to haul goods trucks and reduced costs to 5*d* per train mile.

For three months in 1880 the line saw yet another innovation, two Louis Mekarski compressed-air locomotives brought from France and capable of a speed of 9 mph. They had been built to patents taken out in 1872 and 1873 by Mekarski, concessionaire of the Nantes tramways. Compressed-air locomotives had been first used for hauling construction trains through Alpine tunnels and seemed a very suitable form of motive power for tramways, being clean and quiet. However, the trams failed on two counts: the compressor used almost five times as much coal as a steam locomotive, and the air locomotives could not climb the steep gradient at the end of the return journey to Wantage because their air pressure then was at its lowest.

Tram engine No. 6, designed by James Matthew and built at Kingsbury Works, arrived in 1882. After trials on the tramway, the manufacturers had advertised it for sale, but there were no takers and it lay idle for six years. When the Grantham car started to wear, this Matthew's engine was bought for £60. As No. 6 it gave excellent service for over twenty-five years. With the increase in goods traffic, No. 7, an 0–4–0ST built in 1888 by Messrs T.A. Walker to assist in the construction of the Manchester Ship Canal, was obtained. As its cab was rather open, sacks or tarpaulins were suspended to keep out the cold, wind and rain. Another interesting engine was 0–4–0ST *Raven*. Built by Avonside in 1874, it ran on the broad gauge South Devon Railway, but was constructed for easy conversion to standard gauge. Bought by the Wantage Tramway in 1910, she was scrapped after a collision in 1919. All the engines were painted green.

The tramway had three passenger trailers for haulage by tram engine. No. 1, originally a double-deck horse-drawn car, was converted to single deck for steam haulage; No. 2 was single deck, as was No. 3, purchased in 1890 to replace the Grantham steam car taken out of use that year. In July 1903, two horse-drawn cars rendered redundant by the electrification of Reading Tramways were purchased and became Wantage Nos 4 and 5. Both these cars proved prone to derailment and in 1912 were sold and replaced by two new cars purchased from Hurst, Nelson and Company which retained the earlier numbers. No. 4 was a bogie vehicle and had been exhibited at the first Tramways and Light Railways Exhibition in the Agricultural Hall, Islington Green in 1900 and retained at Hurst, Nelson's works until sold to the Wantage Tramway. No. 5 was a four-wheeler constructed in 1902 for Bradford Corporation but left as spare when the order was cancelled. It had fanciful windows comprising three large panes of bevelled glass on each side, interspersed with narrow vertical lights of different coloured glass. Nos 4 and 5 were probably the only British trams equipped with steam heating. The Wantage Tramway did not own any goods stock, this being provided by coal merchants, other traders or the GWR.

The tramway gave an excellent service, meeting every train stopping at Wantage Road. First and second class compartments were provided until 1 January 1889, after when only one class was offered. Fares were relatively high; 9*d* single in 1928 compared with 2½*d* or 3*d* for a similar distance on an electric tramway.

Goods traffic averaged 500 tons per week, the principal commodities being coal, corn, building materials, groceries and ironmongery. Unlike most branch lines, as opposed to tramways, it flourished. In 1883 32,893 passengers were carried against an estimate of 23,338. In 1900 39,044 passengers were carried and around the turn of the century the company regularly paid a dividend of around 4 per cent. Following the opening of the branch to Lower Yard, Sansum's Row, Wantage, on 18 July 1905 the number of wagons moved annually rose from three thousand to just over five thousand. That year 54,976 passengers were carried and ordinary shareholders received a dividend of 6 per cent from 1903 until 1911. An interesting facility was the teaming on at least one occasion of the tramway, the GWR and the Empire Theatre, Swindon, to issue a 4s 4d ticket to cover travel and admission to a musical comedy.

In the immediate post-First World War period, temporary closure of the flour mill and other reasons caused income to fall, a situation rendered more precarious by W.A. Noble, the tramway's manager for twenty years, absconding in November 1919 with a large sum. Although the goods tonnage improved, passenger traffic declined, particularly with the introduction on 17 October 1924 of a GWR bus service between Wantage Road station and the town. After a few months this competition forced the tramway to withdraw its passenger service on 31 July 1925. Parcels and mail were then carried by the GWR bus.

Locomotives Nos 5 and 7 were retained for goods traffic; the Anglo-American Oil Company, the Cement Marketing Company, Clark's Mill and Wantage Gas Company continued to provide regular traffic in addition to supplies needed by the local coal merchants. The tramway still operated at a profit but little was spent on the permanent way and the locomotives. As an economy measure no fireman was carried, the driver being responsible for this duty. At midday on 8 January 1936, No. 6 and six wagons became derailed near Grove Bridge, blocking the main road until the next morning. Mud thrown on the track by American lorries from the Grove airfield caused the line's temporary closure from November 1943 until February 1944. On reopening locomotive No. 5 was unserviceable and needed repair, while No. 7 also required overhaul but was just about roadworthy, so the number of trips was reduced to two daily, with a maximum load of seven loaded wagons per trip. Eventually No. 7 became unserviceable and operated the tramway's last trip on 21 December 1945. The poor state of the locomotives, coupled with the Oxford Gas Company closing its Wantage gasworks and the increasing wage bills of the tramway, had made the essential replacement of the permanent way quite uneconomic. The line's dismantling started in April 1946, No. 7 helping with this sad task.

When the tramway rolling stock was auctioned on 25 April 1946, No. 5 *Shannon* was purchased by the GWR for £100 for preservation and, after cosmetic restoration, was exhibited on the 'Down' platform of Wantage Road station. Following this station's closure in 1965, she was removed for safe storage to the Wantage Radiation Laboratory, before being moved to the Great Western Society's collection at Didcot in January 1969. On 31 August 1975 at the Grand Steam Cavalcade from Shildon to Heighington in County Durham to celebrate the 150th anniversary of the Stockton and Darlington Railway, No. 5 *Shannon* was the oldest working locomotive.

The Wantage Tramway commenced from an end-on connection with the GWR in its goods yard, a run-round loop being provided for the tramway engines operating passenger services. For most of its length the tramway ran alongside the 25 to 35 ft wide road with no intervening fence. The 45 lb per yd Vignoles rails were bolted directly to longitudinal sleepers, the gauge being maintained by metal tie bars set at intervals. When track was renewed, transverse sleepers were installed. The track was mostly along a tree-lined level road, running along the east side until it reached the outskirts of Wantage. It occupied a width of no more than 6 ft. At the outskirts was a large house, The Elms, where mill owner Tommy Clark lived. In season, trains stopped here to load fruit from his orchard and conveyed it onwards to Covent Garden. By The Elms the lines to the Upper and Lower yards parted, the points being locked and set for the Upper Yard to prevent children altering them. The line to the Upper Yard climbed at 1 in 47 for almost a quarter of a mile past the gasworks. Passenger trains terminated at a platform covered by a train shed, the platform seeming an unnecessary expense as all the passenger cars had steps to facilitate access from ground level. Elsewhere there were no stations, passengers being picked up en route. A cattle dock adjoined the smaller of the two engine sheds and the yard was very cramped.

The Lower Yard was more spacious and close to Clark's flour mill. Flour was sent to Huntley and Palmer's, Serpell's and occasionally Peak Frean's in GWR box vans branded 'Flour Traffic Only. Empty to Wantage Road.' Four vans a day was the normal output, each van taking fifty 2½ cwt sacks. Track in the Lower Yard consisted of Krupps flat-bottomed rail purchased second-hand from the Midland and South Western Junction Railway, W.A. Noble, the tramway manager, being a former employee of that company.

Wantage Engineering Company brought traffic to the line: steel and pig iron inwards, and mining equipment and ploughs outwards, all heavy goods using the Upper Yard where the crane was available.

No guard's van was coupled to the rear of a train, but after dark a red light was hung on the coupling hook of the last wagon. An unofficial use of a Wantage Tramway engine was collecting a slip coach on the GWR main line and drawing it alongside the platform on the rare occasions when a guard misjudged the distance.

The best story about the line regards an engine driver and a one-legged sweep who made a bet in a pub as to whether the sweep's donkey or the tramway locomotive was the fastest. In the event steam failed to triumph over muscle and postcards commemorating the event were sold for many years afterwards. They bore the rhyme:

> A curious race has come to pass
> Between an engine and an ass;
> The Wantage Tram, all steam and smoke
> Was beat by Arthur Hitchcock's moke.

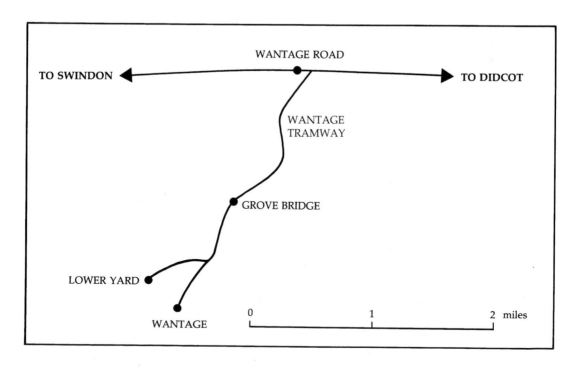

WANTAGE
TRAMWAY

A MEETING

Of Persons favourable to a Tramway Communication between the Town of

Wantage & the Wantage Road Station,

Of the Great Western Railway, will be held at the

TOWN-HALL

IN
WANTAGE,
ON
Wednesday, Oct. 22, 1873

At half-past Three o'clock in the Afternoon.

LT. COL. LOYD LINDSAY, V.C., M.P.

Has kindly consented to preside at the Meeting,

And the Inhabitants of the Town of Wantage and Neighbourhood are earnestly requested to assist in the undertaking.

PRINTERS: J. LEWIS & CO., STATIONERS, &c., WANTAGE.

Notice to call a meeting to form the Wantage Tramway Company.

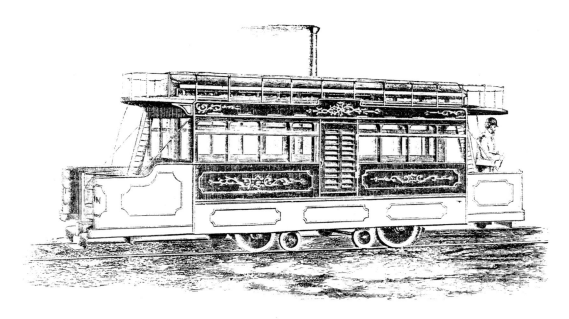

John Grantham's steam tram, the first of its kind in Britain.

Locomotive No. 7 and bogie car No. 4 near Grove Bridge.

1914 Author's collection

Matthew's tram engine No. 6 and bogie car No. 4 at Wantage Road station.

1912 Author's collection

Hughes's tram engine No. 4 and two cars soon after leaving Wantage Road station. The distant hump in the road is the overbridge across the GWR main line.

c. 1900 Author's collection

Cars Nos 3 and 1 and tram engine No. 4 at Wantage Road.

c. 1905 Author's collection

No. 7 (left) draws No. 5, minus its coupling and connecting rods, on its last journey from Wantage to Wantage Road.

1946 Lens of Sutton

Nos 5 and 7 by the 'small' engine shed, Wantage. No. 5 has a sheet to keep out the elements, while No. 7 has a board to perform the same task.

c. 1945 Lens of Sutton

No. 7 shunting at Wantage Road. The upper floor of the GWR station building can be seen on the left, and the bridge carrying the road over the GWR main line is immediately behind the locomotive's chimney.

Lens of Sutton

No. 7 in the Upper Yard, Wantage, shunting coal wagons by the 'large' engine shed and repair shop.

Lens of Sutton

The Wantage Tramway.

Tram engine No. 6 and car No. 3 at Wantage. The man wearing the apron is a curiosity. Among railwaymen, it was generally only carters who wore this form of dress.

c. 1905 Author's collection

Car No. 5 and tram engine No. 6 in the passenger train shed, Wantage.

c. 1905 Author's collection

Tram engine No. 6 and cars No. 5 (left) and No. 3 (right) at Wantage.

c. 1925 Lens of Sutton

Car No. 5 in the passenger train shed at Wantage. The presence of private owners' wagons on the right and the barrow on the platform give the scene a railway, rather than tramway, appearance.

c. 1925 Lens of Sutton

A comic postcard published in September 1925.

Wantage Tramway ticket, *c.* 1925.

No. 5 *Shannon* cosmetically restored and mounted for display at the GWR's Wantage Road station.
16.4.48 Hugh Ballantyne

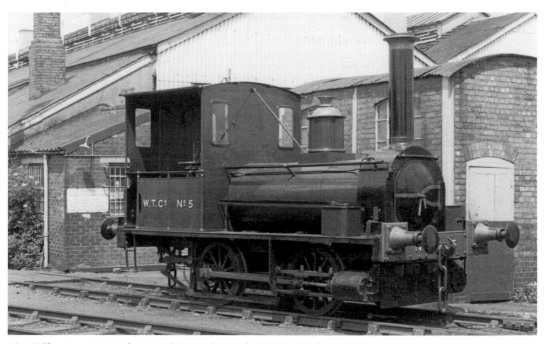

No. 5 *Shannon* restored to working order at the Didcot Railway Centre.

27.6.81 Author

Uffington to Faringdon

The opening of the GWR in 1840 to Faringdon Road, later named Challow, put Faringdon itself into a backwater. To try and redress the balance, the townsfolk pressed for a railway to restore their trade, the necessary Act of Parliament to allow it to be built being granted on 13 August 1860. It authorized the company to raise £22,500 shares and £7,500 in loans. Mr Brodie of Carmarthen was appointed engineer and the tender of Mr Lewis, also of Carmarthen, was accepted to carry out the work of building the line. Construction started early in 1861.

Oriel College, Oxford, was a great help to the railway as it agreed to accept company bonds instead of cash for its land which the line required. Other less generous landowners required hard currency. The East Gloucestershire Railway approached the Faringdon Company with a scheme for a line from Cheltenham to Faringdon, and had this come about it would have improved the company's finances as railways forming through routes, rather than branch lines, paid the highest dividends. In April 1862 work on the line ceased, ostensibly because it was thought prudent to wait until the East Gloucestershire Railway Act was passed in case the line had to be built at a different level, but the real reason was that the Faringdon Railway had run out of funds. This stoppage caused the contractor and engineer to resign. In October the EGR bill was thrown out of Parliament and the Faringdon Railway was left as a short branch line. Following pleadings by the directors, Lewis recommenced the contract on 1 March 1863.

As was unfortunately all too common on railway construction sites, accidents occurred. One young man riding on a muck wagon was jolted off, the wheels crushing his legs. He died while undergoing amputation. A navvy working in a poorly-supported trench had his ribs and collar bone crushed when the sides caved in. He died of his injuries a few days later.

The station buildings at Faringdon were erected by Malachi Bartlett of Witney. Interestingly, the 600 tons of stone he required were sent more cheaply via the circuitous route from Witney via Oxford, Didcot and Uffington, than direct by road. Of unusual design, Faringdon station had two parallel roofs with a massive chimney in the valley gutter. There were Gothic arched doorways and buttressed corners. It was one of the relatively few GWR branch platforms which had the station name on the seats. Faringdon had a large stone-built goods shed.

The line complete, on 13 April 1864 Capt. F.H. Rich made the essential inspection on behalf of the Board of Trade to ensure that the line was safe to be opened to the public. He was not at all impressed. Some bridges were not of a suitable standard; signalling was inadequate; the 70 ft wide level crossing at Uffington was dangerous as there were no gates across the railway to prevent driven animals straying on the track. These matters being corrected, he returned exactly a month later and passed the line.

The Faringdon Railway was opened to the public on 1 June, the day being declared a public holiday, but no specially decorated train was run. The GWR ran four trains each way daily, taking ten minutes for the 3½ mile journey. Three trains ran on Sundays. July saw the number of weekday trains increased to six, with the time allowed being eased to fifteen minutes. The red-brick station at Uffington opened on the same date as the Faringdon line. As it was not intended that branch trains should run direct on to the main line, a trailing siding was provided for freight exchange. The opening of the branch affected the diet of the district, for the rapid transport of sea fish enabled a fishmonger to set up business in Faringdon.

The gauge of the main line from Didcot to Swindon was 'mixed' in February 1872, meaning that the track was adapted to take standard as well as broad gauge rolling stock. As the Faringdon Railway had yet to be converted – the truth was that it could not afford the expense – it meant that no standard gauge wagon could run to Faringdon. To avoid the trouble and expense of transfer from broad to standard gauge at Uffington, outwards goods from Faringdon were taken by road to the main line at Challow. The GWR offered to carry out the track conversion for £102. This accepted, the branch was closed on 26 and 27 July 1878 for the operation to be carried out, trains being temporarily replaced by two horse-drawn coaches taking an hour to cover the distance. Conversion seemed worthwhile when traffic receipts rose. This was the last solely broad gauge branch east of Bristol.

In 1869 Faringdon dispatched about eight milk churns daily, while four years later the figure had increased to about twenty-three. In 1921 milk traffic was carried in a van which left by the 6.15 p.m. passenger train from Faringdon to Uffington, where it was attached to the 6.20 p.m. Swindon to Reading stopping passenger. Eventually reaching Paddington, it returned to Uffington by the 5.33 a.m. Paddington to Swindon, and back to Faringdon by the 8.45 a.m. In a similar way, the station truck from Faringdon was detached at Uffington from the 12.55 a.m. Paddington to Gloucester, worked to Faringdon so that the parcels inside could be delivered to the various shops and businesses. Reloaded, it worked back to Paddington in the evening.

In 1886 the line's directors, realizing that the line would never really pay, sold the undertaking to the GWR. One economy the GWR was able to make was to close the branch on 29 and 30 September 1925 for occupation by the engineer, this being cheaper than him carrying out the work on Sundays when overtime had to be paid. In 1926 H.L. Williams, assistant to the superintendent of the line, was asked to make a report on how costs on the branch could be reduced. He wrote:

Passengers have to change trains which is inconvenient and gives an advantage to road transport. Goods traffic, especially perishables needing a quick transit, stand on sidings waiting a service on the branch or main line and the station is remote from the village, which was not a disadvantage when the line was built, but now gives an advantage to the motor bus. Very little can be done but we will keep an eye on the situation.

Principal traffic on the branch was coal, boards, hay, roadstone and tin boxes. In 1925 Faringdon dealt with an average of twenty-two wagons daily and an annual total of 56,152 milk churns and 370 cattle trucks. Around 1962 1,131 tons of coal were brought in annually.

1923 marked the beginning of the end as far as passenger services were concerned, for that year City of Oxford Motor Services operated a bus from Oxford, and Bristol Tramways and Carriage Company ran buses from Swindon. The last passenger train ran on 29 December 1951.

The branch locomotive was kept in a stone-built shed at Faringdon. Water was supplied from a deep well in the goods yard, and pumped by a stationary engine worked by steam from the locomotive via the whistle connection, the whistle itself being removed. The shed was run by two drivers, two firemen and a cleaner. It closed in 1933 as an economy measure, an engine then travelling from Swindon daily. The building was subsequently converted into a milk depot.

Class 517 0–4–2Ts were the mainstay of the branch, and in the early years of this century hauled a set of three four-wheeled coaches, at one time including two former Hammersmith and City Railway vehicles. 2021 class tank engines of both the saddle and pannier variety worked the branch and from 1945 the single coach was mainly hauled by a 57XX 0–6–0PT. In the freight-only era trains were worked by 0–6–0PTs of the 8750, 94XX and 16XX classes.

Firing an engine on the branch needed skill. As it was only 3½ miles in length, the quantity of steam required had to be carefully judged so that there was sufficient available to surmount the gradient of 1 in 88, but not so much that on arrival the safety valves lifted, wasting steam, coal and causing a noise. The branch locomotive burnt an average of a ton of coal a day, or about 26 lb per mile.

Due to the dip between Uffington and Faringdon, on loose-coupled goods trains, if drivers were not careful to keep the couplings taut going downhill, the wagons buffered up, and as the train started going uphill, the chains jerked straight and weak links could break. This happened on at least one occasion, and the brake van and some wagons see-sawed up and down the dip.

The first diesel engine appeared on 2 January 1962, when the water columns at Faringdon and Uffington were frozen and a 205 hp diesel shunter was substituted for the usual steam engine. The gradient up Barrowbush Hill proved too much for this modern form of traction and the train had to be divided. Next day a tender engine arrived which carried enough water to run from Swindon to Faringdon and back.

An unfortunate accident occurred on the branch in 1916. The permanent way ganger, knowing the timetable, was overconfident and omitted to ask the signalman's permission for his gang to push its trolley towards Faringdon. He was quite unaware that a special was running that day. The train burst into view round a curve, and although the men managed to jump off in time, the ganger himself was run down and killed.

On two occasions the Royal Train, with the Duke of Edinburgh on board, was stabled overnight on the branch. The coping stones had to be removed from the milk dock and branch platform at Uffington to allow the 'Castle' class engine to negotiate the tight curve without fouling.

The branch closed with the withdrawal of freight services on 1 July 1963.

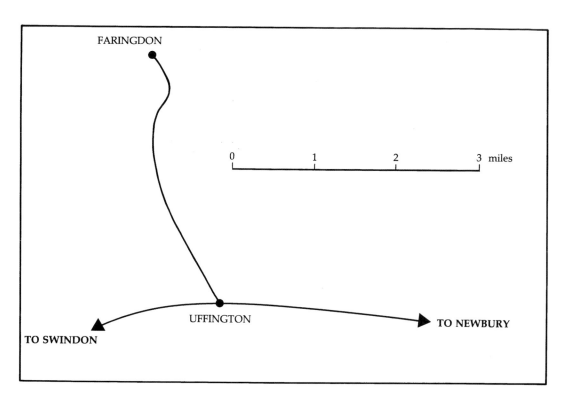

View up the line at Uffington. The name board proclaims 'Uffington Junction for Faringdon'. Note the milk churns standing on both platforms. The footbridge appears to have been designed to cope with any future quadrupling of the main lines.

c. 1919 Lens of Sutton

Uffington after closure of the Faringdon branch to passengers. The name board now simply reads 'Uffington'. The water tower can be seen on the far left and the Faringdon branch can just be discerned on its far side. The station does not look as cared for as in the view taken forty years previously.

c. 1960 Lens of Sutton

Faringdon, the view towards the buffers. On the left are the water tower and locomotive shed. The branch passenger coaches stand at the platform of the station building with two roofs. In the centre is the signal-box hut, while to the right are the goods shed, loading gauge and branch tank engine.

c. 1910 Author's collection

A view from the buffer stops at Faringdon looking towards Uffington. Passenger coaches stand at the platform and the engine can be seen at the far end of the layout running round to the other end of its train. The engine shed is on the right.

27.7.19 Lens of Sutton

This photograph is taken from a similar viewpoint after closure to passenger traffic.

c. 1961 Lens of Sutton

The exterior of Faringdon station on the occasion of an enthusiasts' special visit. The gasworks can be seen on the right.

c. 1960 Lens of Sutton

1361 class 0–6–0ST No. 1365 at Faringdon with a Railway Enthusiasts' Club special. The unusual twin-roofed building is apparent in this view. The loading bank is to the left of the locomotive.

26.4.59 David Lawrence

Newbury to Lambourn

The first scheme for linking Newbury with Lambourn was a horse-drawn tramway put forward in 1873 by E.E. Allen, engineer to the Didcot, Newbury and Southampton Railway. It was anticipated that this form of transport would carry coal for a tenth of the price charged by road. The first rails were ceremonially spiked in Cheap Street, Newbury, by the Mayor of the Borough and the Countess of Craven, but on reaching Donnington Square the undertaking ran into financial difficulties.

In 1881 the scheme was revived as a railway, rather than tramway, and the first sod turned at Welford Park on 18 June 1888, the intervening years being spent trying to raise capital. For the sake of economy, as far as possible the line was built following the lie of the land, but a sizeable cutting by the Bath Road at Speen was required and gave some difficulty to the contractor as the land slipped. The line's ruling gradient was 1 in 60. Two years after the contractor, J.E. Billups of Cardiff, had started, he abandoned the almost completed undertaking. A lawsuit followed, with judgement and damages being given against him.

There then followed six years when nothing was done to the works. The line was eventually completed by S. Pearson and Son, and after Col. Yorke had inspected the railway on behalf of the Board of Trade, the line was opened on Saturday 2 April 1898, a decorated locomotive hauling the first train which comprised four coaches. These had been purchased for a total of £1,300 by the LVR's chairman, Col. Archer-Houblon, the company being so short of funds and having the coaches on hire-purchase from him. In a livery of plain varnished wood with gold lettering, they had a central corridor and open platforms at each end which facilitated the passage of the conductor-guard. The second class seats were wooden. These coaches were sold in 1904, No. 1 going to the Burry Port and Gwendraeth Valley Railway in Wales and the other three to the Hundred of Manhood and Selsey Tramway.

Public traffic started on the Lambourn Valley Railway on 4 April 1898. Four days later a tragedy occurred when two boys were killed at the bridge over the River Kennet on the outskirts of Newbury. The line had remained so long unfinished that it had become a playground. The lads were watching a boat passing under a bridge and as they ran across the line to see it emerge from the other side, they were struck by a train which had silently approached. The driver was so shaken that he never drove again.

For the first six months of operation, the company hired two locomotives from the GWR to work trains, but then the LVR calculated that money could be saved by having its own and bought two 0–6–0Ts for £1,330 each from Messrs Chapman and Furneaux. Bearing tourists in mind, it named them *Aelfred* and *Ealhswith* in honour of King Alfred and his queen. A third locomotive, *Eadweade*, was added in 1903 to avoid hiring an engine from the GWR when the other two were undergoing repair. It was similar to the others but was purchased from Hunslet at a cost of £1225, Chapman's having closed two years previously. The locomotives were painted dark blue and had bright brass number-plates on a scarlet ground. The safety valve casings were of bright brass and the copper chimney caps lovingly polished.

Goods traffic was carried in eighteen second-hand vehicles, six being bought from the GWR for £91 10s and twelve from the Metropolitan Railway Carriage and Wagon Company for £189. These, too, were on hire-purchase from Col. Archer-Houblon.

The LVR went all out to seek traffic and arranged combined rail and coach excursions from London to Lambourn which included lunch, tea and a drive in horse brakes to the site of King Alfred's palace, the Blowing Stone, Wayland's Smithy (familiar to readers of Sir Walter Scott's *Kenilworth*) and White Horse Hill.

In 1900, while the LVR was still an independent company, the GWR investigated the line and found that there was no hope of economizing on staff as all employees worked hard, turning their hand to various duties. At each of the small stations, a lad was employed to carry out all the tasks, including cleaning, parcel delivery and superintending goods traffic. At Lambourn tickets were issued by two girls who also dealt with correspondence. Mr Brain, the station-master, assisted in the yard, 'putting his shoulder to the horse boxes and trucks as required'. He also travelled to Newbury to bank the cash and, on at least one occasion, with the help of a lad, pushed an empty wagon from a siding on to the train.

The LVR found it impossible to run the railway at a profit and in May 1904 an economy was effected by hiring two railmotors from the GWR at a cost of £420 a year. The three locomotives were sold to the Cambrian Railways for £2000, and were taken over by the GWR in 1923 when the Cambrian became a constituent company. In 1931 *Ealhswith* was sold to Mells Collieries Limited, near Frome in Somerset, and eventually scrapped in 1945.

The advent of the railmotors failed to solve the LVR's difficulties and the undertaking was sold to the GWR for £50,000 on 1 July 1905. To gain more traffic the GWR opened a halt at Newbury, West Fields on 1 October 1906 and the following year constructed a passing loop at Welford Park. The ticket office from Welford Park is now preserved at Didcot Railway Centre. Around 1910 a red-brick station building replaced the former timber one at Lambourn and the platform was raised to the standard height instead of the 9 in high LVR pattern. Until 1936, when Lambourn engine shed was closed, two crews plus an overnight engine cleaner were based at the terminus. Locomotives from Didcot were subshedded at Lambourn on a weekly basis.

By 1937 bus competition meant the line was running at a loss, so No. 18, an economical, low-geared diesel railcar, was introduced, capable of carrying passengers and also hauling a few goods wagons or horseboxes. However, No. 18 caused a problem at Lambourn as its horn was similar to that used for alerting the fire brigade, and on at least one occasion, the local firefighters, hearing what they believed was their alarm, turned out. Goods trains, and also passenger trains when the diesel railcar was not functioning, were often handled by one of the three ex-Midland and South Western Junction Railway 2-4-0 tender engines shedded at Reading from 1929 to 1952. On Sunday afternoons it was the duty of the passenger engine to pump water. The whistle was removed and a pipe coupled in its place, thus taking steam to work the donkey engine in a nearby hut. To keep the whistle valve open, a coal pick was hung on the whistle chain.

A considerable proportion of the branch's revenue was derived from the carriage of racehorses, several thousand being carried annually between the training establishments in the area and various race meetings. Some of the horseboxes were specifically allocated to particular trainers whose names appeared on the sides. These vehicles were gaslit, their reservoirs being replenished from a gas tank wagon usually kept in the yard at Lambourn.

In 1954 a 2 mile long branch constructed from Welford Park to the American Air Force depot helped to partly revive the fortunes of the branch. However, passenger trains were withdrawn from 4 January 1960 when the section from Lambourn to Welford Park closed completely, and the track was lifted in 1962. Ten years later the Ministry of Defence worked the line to Welford Park but maintenance costs caused it to be closed and it is believed that the last freight train ran in June 1972. On 3 November 1973, a nine-car DMU worked four return trips over the line, carrying a total of 3,000 passengers, including Mrs J. Puxley, granddaughter of Col. Archer-Houblon. The contractors, Messrs T.W. Ward, commenced track-lifting in 1977; the operation took two months.

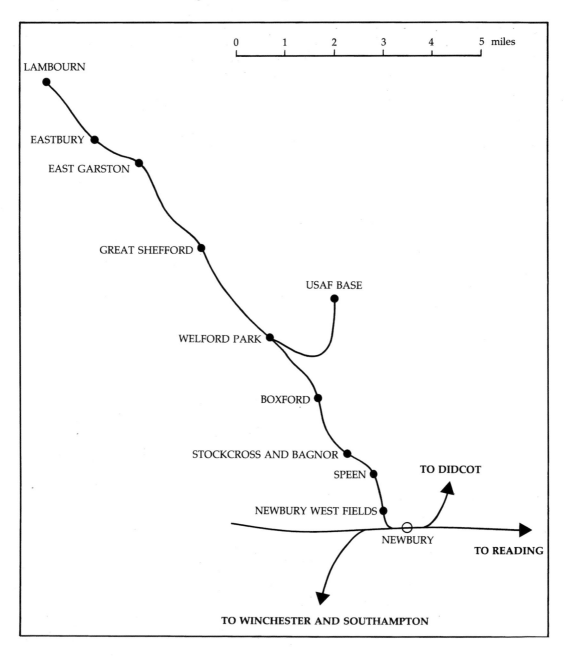

Lambourn Valley Railway.

✦INAUGURAL DINNER,✦

WEDNESDAY, JANUARY 18TH, 1899.

Chairman ... .. REV. R. BAGNALL.

❦ Menu. ❦

Turkey.   Sausages.

Roast Chicken and Bacon.

Ducks.

Veal and Ham.

Boiled Beef.   Roast Beef.

Boiled Leg of Mutton.   Roast Leg of Mutton.

Steak and Kidney Pies.

Veal and Ham Pies.   Rabbit Pies.

———

Plum Puddings.   Mince Pies.

Apple Pies.

Jellies.   Pastry.

———

Cheese and Celery.

W. S BOOTH,

Caterer,

"GEORGE" HOTEL,

LAMBOURN.

Goodman, Printer, Newbury.

The menu for the Inaugural Dinner of the Lambourn Valley Railway.

Lambourn Valley Railway 0–6–0T *Ealhswith* at Newbury. It was built by Chapman and Furneaux.
c. 1900 Author's collection

Lambourn station, with a platform only just above rail level. The view was taken just before rebuilding. The goods shed is on the left and engine shed centre left.
c. 1907 Author's collection

850 class 0–6–0ST No. 1972 at Great Shefford (note that the postcard manufacturer has made a spelling error). In 1915 this engine was fitted with pannier tanks. The auto-trailer is probably No. 8. Behind is a 21 ft van, its roof noticeably lower than the coach. Note the low platform, which was raised to standard height in 1910.

c. 1906 Author's collection

850 class 0–6–0ST No. 2007 at Newbury with a Lambourn train. The clerestory brake vehicle behind the engine was used to supplement the single coach on busier days.

c. 1935 Lens of Sutton

850 class 0–6–0ST No. 2007 with an 'Up' train at Newbury West Fields. The auto-trailer is probably No. 58, which worked on the branch for some time. It was built in 1907 and condemned in 1956.

c. 1935 Lens of Sutton

0–6–0 No. 908, an ex-Cambrian Railways 'Small Goods', heading two clerestory coaches at Lambourn.

c. 1935 Lens of Sutton

850 class 0–6–0ST No. 2007 at Lambourn with strengthening coach and auto-trailer, probably No. 58. This view shows well the exposure of the footplate crew to the elements, and also the tarpaulin which could be drawn over to the uprights to improve their lot slightly. The various fire irons can be seen on the rack above the headlamp.

c. 1935 Lens of Sutton

8750 class 0–6–0PT No. 3728 at Lambourn. The clock under the canopy says 2.42, so this would have been the 2.00 p.m. Newbury to Lambourn service. Note the inspection pit in the foreground marking the position of the former engine shed, and also the white painted bar guarding the point lever.

c. 1957 Lens of Sutton

8750 class 0–6–0PT No. 9791 running round its passenger train. The timber-built signal-box is low on the ground, whereas many such boxes were on a brick base forming the locking room.

c. 1959 T.J. Saunders

8750 class 0–6–0PT No. 4661 running round its coach at Lambourn. The water tower on the left, holding 3,000 gallons, was installed in 1910 at a cost of £160. The gas tank wagon on the right was used for recharging the lighting system of horseboxes. Behind and to the left of this vehicle is a pen made from sleepers placed vertically, and designed to hold locomotive coal.

c. 1957 Lens of Sutton

8750 class 0–6–0PT No. 4670 and auto-trailer arriving at Newbury West Fields with a 'Down' train. Note the platform wall built of sleepers.

c. 1959 Lens of Sutton

The neat halt at Stockcross and Bagnor, looking towards Newbury. The concrete lamppost has a pulley which lowered a hook on which a lighted Tilley lamp was placed before being drawn up by a winding mechanism in the round box near the foot of the post. The seat is of the garden, rather than GWR, variety.

c. 1959 T.J. Saunders

Speen, looking towards Newbury. This is another example of a platform wall built of sleepers, behind which earth was tipped before being topped with gravel.

c. 1959 T.J. Saunders

Ex-GWR railcar No. W18W at Welford Park. It was specially designed for the Lambourn Valley line with couplings and buffers to attach horsebox traffic. The line from the Air Ministry sidings descends behind and in front of the railcar. What looks like a man reading a newspaper is actually the reflection of the name board in the window.

c. 1954 M.E.J. Deane

Railcar No. W18W works the 12.40 p.m. Lambourn to Newbury service. To the left of the door the destination board reads 'Lambourn'.

8.6.54 Hugh Ballantyne

2251 class 0–6–0 No. 2252 at Welford Park returning light engine to Newbury, having worked the 4.10 p.m. passenger ex-Newbury, crosses 57XX class 0–6–0PT No. 7708 with the 5.20 p.m. Newbury to Lambourn.

19.9.59 Hugh Ballantyne

An ex-GWR railcar working the 5.12 p.m. Newbury to Lambourn, crosses 'Dean Goods' No. 2573 at Welford Park. No. 2573 is returning light engine to Newbury after working the 4.15 p.m. Newbury to Lambourn passenger train.

c. 1954 E.C. Griffith

Railcar No. W18W at Welford Park working a Lambourn to Newbury train.

c. 1954 M.E.J. Deane

Passengers leaving Lambourn station, having arrived behind 8750 class 0–6–0PT No. 9791.

c. 1959 T.J. Saunders

Sign preserved at Didcot Railway Centre.

19.8.92 Author

Reading to Sandhurst

The South Eastern Railway reached Reading via a circuitous route. Trains from Cannon Street ran over London, Brighton and South Coast Railway metals from London Bridge to Purley, thence on their own track through Redhill and Reigate to Guildford, while running powers over the LSWR took them on to Ash Junction, where they regained SER rails for the final run to Reading.

The Ash Junction to Reading line was promoted by the Reading, Guildford and Reigate Railway, incorporated on 16 July 1846 to build a 45¾ mile-long line joining Reading with Redhill on the LBSCR, one of the line's objects being to act as a link between Dover and the Midlands. This Act empowered the SER to lease the RGRR at 4½ per cent and half of any profits, though in the event the latter never materialized. Opened on 4 July 1849, the company was absorbed by the SER in 1852.

The original intention of the RGRR was to work the line on the atmospheric system, but fortunately for the shareholders this idea was abandoned. The atmospheric principle was tried out between Exeter and Newton Abbot in 1848 by the South Devon Railway but proved a disaster. A 15 in diameter cast-iron pipe in which a piston travelled was laid between the rails, stationary steam pumps exhausting air from it. To enable the piston to be connected to a special carriage to which a train could be coupled, the top of the pipe had a continuous slit closed by a leather flap. One edge of this longitudinal valve formed a hinge, while the other was smeared with grease to make it airtight, a roller behind the piston resealing the valve. The air in front of the piston being pumped out, atmospheric pressure behind the piston thrust toward it, the carriage to which it was connected and the train coupled behind, leaving the valve closed and the pipe ready to be exhausted for the next train. Primitive technology caused the system's downfall. The leather valve failed to make an airtight seal; the leather itself deteriorated and the pumping engines proved inefficient and unreliable.

On 9 July 1856 the LSWR opened a line from Ascot to Wokingham, using running powers over the SER's branch to reach Reading. This meant that Reading was now served by no less than three railways: the GWR from Paddington, 36 miles; the LSWR from Waterloo, 43½ miles; and the SER from Charing Cross, 68¾ miles. Despite the disparity in distance, the GWR was not the obvious choice and severe competition sprang up between the three companies. Fares were reduced and the SER even collected goods by road from as far afield as Newbury. Uneconomic competition was ameliorated somewhat in 1858 when a three-year agreement was entered into for sharing traffic, fares to London being the same by all routes, charged at 36 miles regardless of the actual distance. All fares were pooled, the GWR receiving two-thirds of passenger revenues from the three companies, and the SER and LSWR two-thirds of the combined goods revenue. An outcome of this agreement was the construction of a double-track spur linking the SER and GWR at Reading. Three chains of this belonged to the SER, 13 chains to the

GWR and the intervening 5 chains was a completely detached property of the LSWR whose own line ended at Wokingham, 6¾ miles from Reading. This connecting spur opened to goods traffic on 1 December 1858 and to passengers on 17 January 1859. A shorter and better placed junction line than this through the goods yard was opened on 17 December 1899, while yet another connecting spur was put in on 1 June 1941. The first two links with the GWR closed on 30 April 1979 and 4 April 1965 respectively, but the third link is still open and receives much use.

The RGRR station at Reading was a small, single, 180 ft long platform at North Forbury Road. It, and the adjacent carriage storage road, was covered by a train shed. Unlike most so-called temporary stations, it really did live up to its name. Work on a new station 300 yd further west, and almost alongside that of the GWR, began in March 1855 and was opened on 30 August 1855. A timber train shed covered a central two-faced platform. On 26 June 1859 it was struck by lightning and caught fire. Rebuilding was completed in the summer of 1860, the platform being lengthened and a new station entrance building provided. On 26 December 1896 a second platform was opened, giving the station four faces in total; the train shed was removed and the platforms had individual awnings. On 26 September 1949 the station was renamed Reading Southern and on 11 September 1961 changed to Reading South.

Reading saw its first electric train service on 1 January 1939, when electric trains from Reading to Waterloo replaced the steam services, but steam continued on the line to Sandhurst. The last scheduled steam-hauled passenger train to leave Reading South was the 10.40 p.m. to Guildford on 3 January 1965, headed by U class 2–6–0 No. 31809, though due to diesel failures, steam engines substituted almost till the end of 1965.

It was decided to make an economy by closing Reading South and concentrate all services on Reading General, the former GWR station. The 1899 connection was electrified so that trains could be taken to the new bay Platform 4A at Reading General. Reading South closed on 6 September 1965. The method of working Platform 4A was most unusual. An electric train from Waterloo ran in followed by a DEMU from Tonbridge, and if the Waterloo train was eight coaches in length, the Tonbridge train was forced to wait outside the station until it departed. As such delays could not be tolerated, on 5 May 1975 an independent Platform 4B was built for Tonbridge trains. At one time Reading South had a large goods yard; the siding to the gasworks was taken out of use on 22 September 1970, and Huntley and Palmer's siding closed on 30 April 1979.

At Earley station, opened in 1863 (fourteen years after the line itself), as insufficient land was available for a normal pattern station, to reduce the area required, the domestic upper floor above the station offices on the 'Down' platform was given an unusual overhanging storey with access via an iron spiral staircase. This upper floor, which has typical SER board cladding, doubles as a platform canopy. When the station closed to goods on 6 January 1969, the oil depot sidings opened c. 1966 remained open.

Winnersh Triangle station was inaugurated on 22 May 1987 to serve new housing and commercial development. As it was situated on an embankment across the Loddon Valley, the platforms were constructed of timber to give a minimum weight.

Sindlesham and Hurst Halt opened on 1 January 1910, but changed its name to Winnersh Halt on 6 July 1930. Its original timber platforms were later replaced by ones made from concrete sections cast at the Exmouth Junction depot. In 1987 the station was further improved by having its platforms lengthened and the original buildings replaced by new structures.

The first station building at Wokingham, which had steeply-sloping roofs and tall chimney-stacks, was replaced by a low, flat-roofed structure in November 1973. The public foot-bridge, originally built from old double-headed rails, and a curved, graceful structure, was replaced by a modern angular design. The goods yard was extended in 1942 but closed on 6 January 1969. An economy was made on 23 April 1933 when the signal-box at the west end of the cattle pens, and the junction signal-box were replaced by one new box on the junction side of the line. At the junction south of the station, the line to Crowthorne goes straight ahead, while that to Bracknell curves left.

The first station at Crowthorne opened on 29 January 1859 and was named Wellington College, like its successor half a mile north, until the latter received its present name on 17 June 1928. The college was established as a memorial to the Duke of Wellington for the education of the sons of deceased army officers. A long siding was made to carry construction materials for the building. The station closed to goods on 3 August 1964, but in more recent times a brick-built shelter has been erected on the 'Down' platform as part of a job-creation scheme.

Sandhurst Halt, opened in June 1852 and closed in December 1853, was reopened in 1909 with timber platforms and wooden waiting shelters. Just over half a mile beyond, and shortly before the siding which served Patterson's gravel pit until it was taken out of use on 7 September 1937, the line crossed the River Blackwater and entered Hampshire.

Through trains from Charing Cross or Cannon Street to Reading were arranged to suit local needs, rather than to cater for the few through passengers. In 1918 about twelve such trains ran daily, taking an average of 3 hours 10 minutes, compared with 1 hour 30 minutes via the LSWR route and 50 minutes by the GWR. However, apart from local traffic, the line is now becoming important as part of a through route between Reading and Dover, and this importance will grow with the development of Continental traffic due to the opening of the Channel Tunnel.

At first the line was not favoured as a through route, due to the break of gauge at Reading, but through services from the Midlands to Kent and Sussex resorts began in 1897. In order to carry passengers over its lines for the maximum mileage, the South Eastern and Chatham Railway, as the SER had become, publicized Reading as being useful as an exchange point for passengers from Dover to the Midlands and North, and in 1907 ran an express service from Dover to Reading in 3 hours 21 minutes. The use of this route meant passengers avoided having to cross London. The SECR *Official Guide* for 1907 stated:

> Sufficient time is usually allowed at Reading for passengers to partake of substantial refreshments before joining the trains which proceed northward through Oxford, Leamington, Birmingham and Wolverhampton to Crewe and Manchester; to Shrewsbury and Aberystwyth, Llangollen and Barmouth. And also via Chester to Birkenhead, Liverpool and Manchester.

In the 1950s six to eight through trains ran on summer Saturdays, but these were withdrawn on 5 September 1964. Today the line has thirty-six stopping trains each way – about one every thirty minutes. All go to Guildford, with approximately every other one running through to Gatwick Airport. Four trains are provided through to and from Tonbridge. Long-distance passenger services comprise Manchester to Brighton and Edinburgh to Brighton trains. In recent years through mail trains have been introduced: three to Dover from Bristol, Crewe and Manchester and two to Redhill from Northampton and Preston.

The two-road brick engine shed at Reading, situated south of the line, was replaced with a three-road brick shed erected in the 1860s at the foot of the GWR embankment. The two-road shed was retained and used as a goods depot, and later a bonded warehouse, until demolished in the early 1970s. Until the 1923 Grouping, one line was always reserved for visiting LSWR engines. The SECR itself stabled about twenty engines at Reading. In 1933 the stud consisted of twenty-two engines, almost half of which were F1 class 4–4–0s allocated to Waterloo workings, but after electrification this number was reduced to seventeen. In the 1950s the shed had F1s, R1s and a few Maunsell 2–6–0s. In May 1954 only two engines remained, both shunters; the remainder had been transferred to Redhill and Guildford. In December 1956 the shunters were placed in store. Reading shed became a 'sub' of Basingstoke in 1957, and of Guildford the following year. It was completely closed in January 1965. Three engines once shedded at Reading have been preserved:

U class 2–6–0 No. 31618 on the Bluebell Railway
U class 2–6–0 No. 31806 on the Mid Hants Railway
D class 4–4–0 No. 31737 at the National Railway Museum, York.

From 1938 GWR locomotives worked certain trains over the branch en route from Reading to Redhill. However, from 4 January 1965 the stock used on Reading to Tonbridge trains has been a diesel-electric multiple-unit motor and trailer coach designed for the severely restricted gauge Hastings line and only 8 ft 0¾ in wide plus a standard width control tailer. This combination of two narrow coaches and a wider vehicle caused the sets to be nicknamed 'Tadpoles', as from the air they resembled these creatures. Only the two ex-Hastings coaches were equipped with corridor connections, and when the economical conductor-guard working began on 5 November 1967 the compartments in the non-corridor control tailer were locked except at peak periods.

Two companies at Reading had their own industrial locomotives. Until rail traffic ceased in 1976, Reading Gasworks latterly used two 0–4–0DM engines built by John Fowler and Company. Huntley and Palmer's biscuit factory initially used two Black, Hawthorn and Company 0–4–0STs, joined by two similar Peckett engines in 1900; unusually, these four engines were lettered instead of numbered. In 1932 two W.G. Bagnall 0–4–0 fireless locomotives appeared, charged with steam from a stationary boiler. Rail traffic on these private sidings ceased in December 1969.

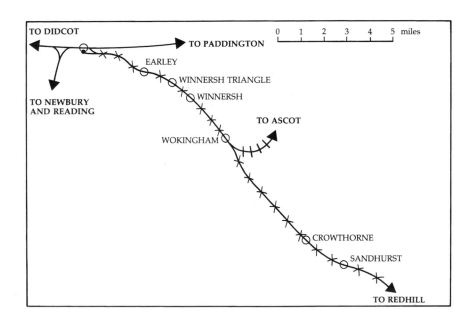

The Reading, Guildford and Reigate Railway station at Reading on the right, with the GWR station to the left and at a higher level.

c. 1850 Author's collection

Reading, showing left to right: goods shed, locomotive shed and passenger shed.

c. 1852 George Measom

Reading, Guildford and Reigate Railway bridge over the Bath Road, Reading.

c. 1850 Author's collection

A Reading, Guildford and Reigate Railway goods train about to cross the bridge over the River Kennet at Reading.

c. 1850 Author's collection

A Reading, Guildford and Reigate goods train crossing the bridge over the River Loddon east of Earley.

c. 1850 Author's collection

Reading stations from the air: SR centre, GWR lower.

c. 1925 M.E.J. Deane collection

The exterior of the ex-SER station at Reading, the original building being in a domestic style. The modern flat-roofed extension blends fairly well with the original.

c. 1958 Lens of Sutton

The platform side of Reading Southern station. The clock tower of Reading General station can be seen in the upper right. Note the modern phenomenon of the appearance of litter.

c. 1958 Lens of Sutton

U class 2–6–0 No. 31801 (shed-plate 71A, Eastleigh) at Reading South, heading the 2.50 p.m. to Redhill.

6.6.64 E. Wilmshurst

N class 2–6–0 No. 31862 (75B, Redhill) has arrived at Reading Southern with a train from Redhill, the set being No. 218. An engine has been coupled on to the other end ready for the return journey. The wooden trough guarding the conductor rail can be clearly seen.

c. 1958 P.Q. Treloar

U class 2–6–0 No. 31809 (70D, Eastleigh) at Reading Southern with the 0945 to Redhill.
24.10.64 Hugh Ballantyne

Reading shed with, left to right: S15 class 4–6–0 No. 30824; N class 2–6–0 No. 31823; and U class 2–6–0s Nos 31620 and 31801.

6.6.64 E. Wilmshurst

S11 class 4–4–0 No. 30400 at Reading Southern with a train to Redhill.

August 1954 Frank J. Saunders

Reading Southern, the view towards the buffer stops. An electric train to Waterloo is on the left, while class 2 2–6–2T No. 41287 heads a train to Redhill on the right. Traffic at this time of day did not warrant the lengthy platforms.

c. 1960 Lens of Sutton

Earley station, looking towards Reading. Note the protruding upper floor providing a platform canopy and saving ground space. The tall starter signal has a repeater arm lower down its post.

c. 1910 Author's collection

U class 2–6–0 No. 31800, rebuilt from 2–6–4T *River Cray*, near Earley with a Redhill–Reading train. Note the break in the conductor rail at the sleeper crossing. The first coach is an ex-SECR 'Birdcage' design, so-called because of its roof being raised at the end to form a guard's lookout.

August 1954 Frank J. Saunders

The building on the 'Down' platform at Earley.

29.12.92 Author

The shop-like ticket office situated at the foot of the embankment, with the platform above.

29.12.92 Author

H16 class 4–6–2T No. 30520 passes Winnersh Halt with an 'Up' freight.

August 1954 Frank J. Saunders

'Austerity' Q1 class 0–6–0 No. 33010 passes Winnersh Halt with an 'Up' freight.

August 1954 Frank J. Saunders

N class 2–6–0 No. 31862 enters Wokingham with the 1.50 p.m. Reading to Guildford service.

6.6.64 E. Wilmshurst

Wokingham. S15 Class 4–6–0 No. 30824 with an 'Up' train passes N class 2–6–0 No. 31408 with the 1.35 p.m. Redhill to Reading service.

6.6.64 E. Wilmshurst

The station building at Wokingham erected in 1973 in the modern style, and with far less architectural character than the original. Class 423 4–VEP EMU No. 3158 is working the 0927 Waterloo to Reading train.

29.12.92 Author

'Wellington College for Crowthorne'; an unidentified engine arrives from Reading and passes below the road and foot-bridges. The station building has the characteristics of a mansion. Note the mountain of trunks near the name board. The timber shed on the right is a parcels lock-up.

c. 1905 Author's collection

A 'Down' train arrives at the timber-platformed Sandhurst Halt. Each platform has two buildings: one is a waiting shelter, and the light-coloured building a ticket office. Each platform is approached by its own path from the under-line bridge.

c. 1912 Author's collection

Reading to Ascot

On 8 July 1853 the Staines, Wokingham and Woking Junction Railway was incorporated to build a line from the Windsor branch at Staines to the SER's Reading line at Wokingham. The promoters were not really aiming at Reading, hoping eventually to reach Oxford, but this dream never came to fruition. The line from Staines to Ascot opened on 4 June 1856 and onwards to Wokingham on 9 July 1856, too late for the SER to have a share in that year's Ascot race meeting traffic. The *Reading Mercury* of 12 July reported:

> On Wednesday morning this line was opened, but the carriages went off with some very light loads; this, we apprehend, may be attributable to the scale of fares, which, as regards the transit from Reading to London exceeds that of the Great Western and nearly doubles that of the South Eastern. It is true that the distance from Reading to Waterloo Bridge is accomplished in rather under two hours, which may be great accommodation to some, as the tedious omnibus travelling is avoided from Paddington to the Strand.

The line from Staines to Wokingham was worked from the start by the LSWR, that company leasing it from 25 March 1858 for 50 per cent of the gross receipts and purchasing it twenty years later.

The section from Reading to Wokingham has already been described in the previous chapter. Three miles east of Wokingham the Binfield Brick and Tile Company's siding just east of Amen crossing was taken out of use on 15 August 1965. Bracknell had a low, single-storey building, and extensive goods sidings which closed on 6 January 1969, though private siding traffic continued until the following year. The passenger station was developed in 1975 and the station offices are now on the ground floor of a multi-storey block on the 'Up' platform.

Martins Heron station opened on 3 October 1988 at a cost of £½m, shared by BR and Berkshire County Council. The unsheltered platforms at Ascot West were used by race traffic from the Reading direction until about 1968 and, not surprisingly, a horse dock was provided. At one time there were also private sidings serving the Laurence Brick Company, and during the First World War sidings were laid to serve the Royal Flying Corps.

Ascot station is situated at the trailing junction with the Bagshot line. Originally it had three platforms serving the Reading lines and two for those to Bagshot. In October 1938 a new track layout was brought into use, with three platforms signalled for reversible working. This meant that any platform was available to Bagshot trains, and three for those to Reading. On 8 September 1974 the layout was rationalized by reducing the station to three platforms, all for two-way working.

A locomotive turntable was provided in the smallish goods yard north-west of the passenger station, and an engine shed to the south-west of the station layout. This rather unusual feature of having turntable and shed separated by the station grew up because the first engine facility was the 40 ft diameter turntable installed in the goods yard, later replaced by a 50 ft table and a small, one-road engine shed. Around 1880 a new, larger single-road shed built of timber was provided but had to be at the opposite end of the station due to lack of room in the goods yard. The turntable in the goods yard was retained and the site of the original engine shed used for building a goods shed. By 1936 the locomotive shed was only used by one engine daily, and as it was not economical to repair the structure, it was closed in 1937. East of the station, sidings served Drake and Mount's, and Ascot and District Gas Company.

Ascot saw much race traffic, and for the June 1905 meeting the LSWR erected a cover over the footpath between the station and the racecourse. In 1910 a single timber-built platform without a shelter was erected on the 'Up' line west of the station to deal with passengers from the Royal Enclosure, access being by footpath through the woods.

The number of trains running over the Ascot to Wokingham branch steadily increased as the population of the area grew. In 1887 the service provided eight trains each way daily; in 1910, fourteen; in 1938, twenty; and in 1993, forty.

The line was electrified to Reading on 1 January 1939, a new service of thirty-six electric trains running from Reading to Waterloo replacing twenty steam services. Trains consisted of 2-BIL units, reducing the journey time to Waterloo by about eleven minutes. These units consisted of two cars, each with a side corridor and lavatory. Two 2-BIL sets coupled together left Waterloo and were split at Ascot, one running to Reading and the other to Camberley and Aldershot, being re-united on the return journey.

Until the 1870s brakes on passenger trains were quite primitive – just a handbrake on the locomotive's tender and a handbrake in the guard's van, or vans if there was more than one guard. In an emergency a driver used his deep-toned whistle to alert the guard to apply his brakes. In due course the government insisted on continuous brakes operating throughout the train on all coaches. The LSWR carried out trials of the automatic vacuum brake on the Reading branch and it was the system ultimately adopted by that company in 1881.

Unlike most other railway companies which used their locomotive headlamps to indicate the class of train, the LSWR used it to show the route. In 1892 Waterloo to Reading trains carried a lamp or disc each side of the smokebox. In 1901 this code was only used for those running between Waterloo and Reading direct. Those via the Virginia Water Curve displayed a lamp or disc in front of the chimney and a diamond on the right-hand side of the smokebox as seen from the front, though in 1921 this was altered to a solitary lamp or disc in front of the chimney. Trains from Waterloo via the Loop line carried a lamp or disc on the left-hand side of the smokebox. The Southern Railway, as successor to the LSWR, continued the system, using it on all its routes. Trains from Reading to Margate via Redhill, and Woking to Reading via Virginia Water West Curve, carried a lamp or disc in front of the chimney; those from Waterloo to Reading via Twickenham carried a lamp or disc on the left of the smokebox, while those via the Loop Line carried a lamp or disc on either side of the smokebox.

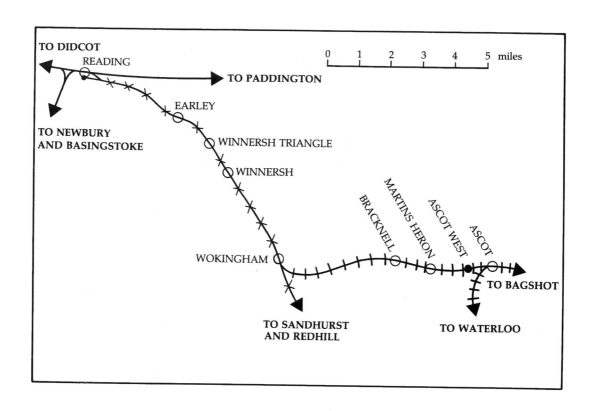

SECR F1 class 4–4–0 No. 1140 leaves Reading for Waterloo. The coach behind the tender is an ex-LSWR vehicle.

c. 1931 M.E.J. Deane collection

Platforms 4A and 4B at Reading, showing class 423 4–VEP EMU No. 7779 with the 12.00 Reading to Waterloo train on the right, and DMU L580, comprising class 119 Nos 51066, 59425 and 51094 working the 12.15 service from Reading to Redhill.

13.6.86 Author

The original single-storey station at Bracknell looking in the 'Up' direction.

c. 1960 Lens of Sutton

The temporary 'Up' platform at Bracknell which was used while the new station and tower block were under construction on the site of the original station. A temporary foot-bridge gives access to the 'Down' platform, largely unaffected by the building works.

1975 Lens of Sutton

Bracknell, the 'Up' view, showing the tower block.
29.12.92 Author

The well-used Bracknell station. As it was mid-morning, the passengers were probably going to or from the post-Christmas sales.

29.12.92 Author

The ticket office on the 'Up' platform at Martins Heron.

29.12.92 Author

Ascot West, looking in the 'Down' direction. The horsebox sidings are on the left, and the military siding diverges to the left beyond the signal-box.

c. 1950 Lens of Sutton

The view of the site of Ascot West from almost the same standpoint as the previous plate, the buildings and platform faces having been removed and Nature taking over.

29.12.92 Author

Up Reading line dock siding and up branch line dock siding.—Bogie coaches must not be shunted alongside these docks.

BRACKNELL.

Maidenhead Brick and Tile Company's siding.—Wagons for the siding will be propelled on the down line, with a brake van as the leading vehicle, from Bracknell station and crossed to the up line at Manor siding box, which will be opened as a block section as required.

Wagons for the siding must be exchanged immediately inside the gate.

Binfield Brick and Tile Company's siding.—Traffic will be exchanged on the portion of the siding adjoining the cart road which extends in a westerly direction from a point approximately 60 feet inside the gate.

A board is provided at the siding warning persons to stand clear of the gate posts at the entrance to the siding when shunting operations are in progress, this being necessary owing to the restricted clearances.

WOKINGHAM.

Lawrence's siding.—The normal position of the hand points leading to the siding will be for the lay-by siding and they must be padlocked in that position when not required to be used for the working of traffic to or from the private siding. The key of the padlock must be kept in Wokingham signal box.

Guards detaching wagons must place them in the right-hand siding inside the gate. Should this siding not be long enough to accommodate all wagons put off, the remainder must be placed in the down lay-by siding running parallel with the main line in the direction of Crowthorne, but wagons are not to be put into this siding for Messrs. Lawrence and Co's yard unless absolutely necessary. Outgoing wagons will be placed in the left-hand siding or loop line inside the gates.

In working this siding special care must be exercised on account of the sharp gradient falling towards the brickyard and public road, and on no account are wagons to be loose shunted.

Guards must see that the loop on Messrs. Lawrence & Co's siding is clear of wagons at the lower end to admit of loaded wagons being drawn from the brickyard into the loop.

All wagons put into this siding must have a sufficient number of brakes pinned down to prevent the wagons running away.

Engines must not proceed beyond the clearance of the points leading to the private siding.

READING.

Reading Gas Company's sidings.—The High Level sidings consist of two reception roads. A catch road is provided at the clearance point of the siding and the points controlling this road are worked from the Gas Works siding ground frame.

Ingoing and outgoing wagons are exchanged on either of the reception roads as required.

Internal movements of wagons are performed by the Gas Company's employees by means of a capstan, and such movements must not take place when the Railway Company's engine is working on the sidings.

The height above rail level of the girder at the entrance to the retort house to which the High Level sidings give access is 9 feet 9 inches only, and great care must be exercised in shunting high-sided wagons, tank wagons, etc., towards the retort house in order to avoid such vehicles coming in contact with this girder.

High-sided and tank wagons must not be shunted into the retort house.

The return trip must be propelled to Reading on the down running line, a competent man riding in the brake van, which must be the leading vehicle.

Wagons may be exchanged on any of the Low Level sidings except the coke hopper spur siding.

The Railway Company's engines must not, on any account, pass under the coke hopper, neither must any attempt be made to couple or uncouple wagons when they are standing beneath the hopper, as there is insufficient space for the purpose.

Wagons may be placed under the hopper by the shunting engine provided there are sufficient wagons between those to be placed under the hopper and the engine to obviate the engine going under the hopper or any uncoupling being done as mentioned in the preceding paragraph, otherwise the movement of wagons in the coke hopper spur will be carried out by the Reading Gas Company's staff.

'Instructions governing the Working of Stations.' From the S.R. Working Timetable appendices, 1934.

Station	Turntables (Length of Rail)		Cranes or runways to lift				Weighbridges			Highway vehicle docks	Water columns	
	Engine	Wagon	Outside		Inside		Truck		Cart		No.	Where situated
	ft. ins.	ft. ins.	T. cwts.	Ht. of lift ft. ins.	cwts.	Ht. of lift ft. ins.	Capacity Tons	Lth. in ft.	Capacity Tons			
Ascot	49 9	—	5 0*	25 0	30	11 6	—	—	—	1	6	All platforms and one near tank
Bracknell ...	—	—	7 10	23 0	30	12 0	—	—	10 (C)	2	—	—
Wokingham ...	—	—	8 0B	19 3	40	15 10	15	13	—	1	—	—
			4 11A	21 9								
Earley	—	—	—	—	—	—	—	—	—	1	—	—
Reading ...	64 10	—	15 0	26 0	30*	14 4	20	18	15 (D 3½)	2	4	Down goods sidings ; Nos. 1 and 2 platfms ; loco depot (2)

'Accommodation and Equipment at Stations.' From the S.R. Working Timetable appendices, 1934.

Name of siding.	Position.	(1) Station in charge of working. (2) wagons labelled to.†	Gradient at point of connection (1 in)	Catch points provided in sidings at.	Points of siding controlled by or worked from.	If gates provided across siding — Key to be obtained from.	Key to be returned to.	Worked by.	Remarks.
Lawrence's ...	Down side between Ascot and Bracknell	Ascot	300 falling towards Bracknell	—	Ascot West Station box	Employees of Messrs. Lawrence		Down goods services	Wagons to be exchanged in Ascot West sidings. *
Maidenhead Brick and Tile Company	Up side between Wokingham and Bracknell	Bracknell	121 falling towards Wokingham	—	Manor Siding box	Bracknell Station Master		Various goods services	For working instructions see page 34. *
Binfield Brick and Tile Co.	Up side between Wokingham and Bracknell	Bracknell	132 falling towards Bracknell	—	Amen Crossing box	Gate controlled by Amen Crossing box		Various goods services	For working instructions see page 34. *
Reading Gas Company (High Level)	Down side between Earley and Reading (connected with Up line)	Reading	147 falling towards Reading	—	Ground frame standard electrical release from Reading Jct.	—	—	Special services	For working instructions see pages 34, 35. *
Reading Gas Company (Low Level)	Down side between Earley and Reading	Reading	Level	At clearance point with main line	Reading Jct. box	—	—	Special services	For working instructions see pages 34, 35. *
Huntley and Palmer	Down side Reading	Reading	Level	—	Hand points from No. 2 siding	—	—	Shunting engine	* —

'List of Intermediate and Other Sidings.' From the S.R. Working Timetable appendices, 1934.

Ascot station from the air, looking towards London. The Reading lines are the three on the left, the two on the right being those to Bagshot. The goods yard is on the right at the far end of the station.

Lens of Sutton